MW01059396

"This book is chock full of practical ideas you can use to overcome obstacles to success. It is a must read for anyone with big goals who wants to find new drive and enthusiasm to get beyond the barriers. You won't be able to put it down!"

—Meloney Sallie-Dosunmu, global director of training and development, Thermo Fisher Scientific

"If you want to find your passion again and live your life with enthusiasm and purpose and move away from what others think it should be, this book is for you. *The No Excuse Guide to Success* gets into your heart, ears and soul and literally challenges you to live life on your own terms and take responsibility for, and advantage of, the God-given talents you have held on 'hold' for so long. After reading this book, your life will never be the same—and will only be much better—no matter what. You won't put this book down from the minute you pick it up. A true 'must read' for life!"

—Andrea Nierenberg, president/CEO, Nierenberg Consulting Group, LLC

"Jim inspires and 'stretches' us to mold to our best!"

—Carolyn Devanayagam, account director and practice lead, Weber Shandwick

"This is an easy book to read. Like Jim's other books, the anecdotes kept me engaged and were educational. His energy and enthusiasm come through in the words on the page."

—Renie McClay, global learning consultant, Inspired Learning LLC

"Anyone who has ever worked with Jim, or heard him speak, knows that his energy and attitude are infectious.

What this inspirational book provides is some insight into his mindset and the mind-set of other successful people. Success is the result of a discipline of thought, choices, and action. Jim outlines a solid process in this book to get your thinking, choices, and action on the path to success. The real-life examples and stories he uses bring his advice to life and make it relatable and practical for the reader. If you need to boost your spirits, redirect your thinking, or just a positive kick in the pants, this book is for you!"

—Theresa Hummel-Krallinger, U.S. director, organizational development and training, Almac Group

"A must read. Jim 'Mr. Energy' Smith brings together a keen understanding of the way we think, dream and live. His approach is practical and insightful. If you are interested in moving from 'fizzle' to 'sizzle,' run and get this book. You won't be disappointed."

—Leslie Shields, The Wiz of Biz, and president, The Chevannes Global Group

"Jim Smith, Jr.'s book is an invaluable lesson for us all that if you want success, you need only study the behaviors of those who habitually say 'can do' versus those who habitually say 'can't do.' Excuses are the ultimate road block to 'reaching higher,' which is why so many people never improve themselves, never improve their business, and never improve their relationships."

—Carsten Pedersen, managing partner, Patriot Benefits Group

"In this book Jim shows you how to go from 'interested' in winning to 'committed' to winning—no matter what. It will change your perspective, your approach, and your life for the better—in business and beyond."

—Deana Poole, top sales performer, Greater Media Philadelphia

"I am one of the people who is blessed to be close to Jim as a trainer and friend in my heart—a place where distance is never an issue. The connection and transformation that Jim knows how to achieve in humans is a true gift. Also in this book, Jim triggers the reader to take responsibility of his/her own life and opportunities. A book you must read, cherish and belongs on your bookshelf."

—Bionda Honig, managing partner, Credit
Management Instituut BV, the Netherlands

"Jim's enthusiasm is infectious...he's absolutely phenomenal when it comes to motivating a room full of people! This book will do the same for you. It'll be like having Jim in your room whenever you want or need him!"

—Sha Batt, field sales training manager-EBU,
Actelion Pharmaceuticals U.S., Inc.

"Jim is Mr. High Impact in the training room and in delivering keynote sessions. He proves it once again with his high-impact writing skills. This is a high-impact book, practical, lively, and relevant to the busy everyday executive. Jim shows you how you can get things done, stop making excuses, take personal responsibility, live your life productively and happily. His honesty in sharing personal life stories makes this book different and stands out as one of the best."

—R. Palan PhD, chairman and CEO,
SMR Technologies, Malaysia

"Jim's passion to be your coach and help you achieve the most out of your life rings throughout this book. The techniques he shares are practical, insightful and inspirational in making change happen."

—Kelly Brantner, executive director, Asian Operations
Rutgers Business School, Beijing, China

"Over the past 10 years, I've read over 1,200 books on sales, marketing, leadership, and success. And Jim Smith, Jr. simply nails it in one incredibly well-thought-out, approachable, and inspiring volume.

Shocking truth #1: Don't read this book—unless you want success!

Shocking truth #2: Why? Because so much of the news is not good. Smith makes sure to show you in no uncertain terms how *you* are responsible, accountable, and in charge of your own success. Forget about excuses, finger-pointing, blame, and psychodrama. He'll call you on all of it. But then like a great sports coach, he will also help pull you up by your bootstraps and show you *exactly* how to improve your game, step by step, day by day, tactic by tactic.

REALITY CHECK: This is not easy, folks! But if you're not discouraged by Smith's "Real Deal" approach, then this is the #1 go-to book for personal and professional success. It's chock-full of tools, application exercises, and fill-in forms to help you translate his wise advice into immediate action.

All of Jim's ideas are actionable, honest, and specific. No sugarcoating and no fluff. As I said, don't read this book. Rather, *use* this book—devour it, dog-ear it, highlight it, write notes in the margins and plaster this puppy with Post-It notes because you'll need every strategy, every idea, every tactic, and every great piece of advice that Jim shares if you're going to be successful in your business career. With Jim at your side, your chances of success just went WAY UP!!!"

—David Newman, author of *Do It! Marketing* and past president, National Speakers Association, Philadelphia

# The No Excuse Guide to Success

# The No Excuse Guide to Success

## No Matter What Your Boss—or Life— Throws at You

By Jim "Mr. Energy" Smith, Jr.

This edition first published in 2012 by Career Press, an imprint of
Red Wheel/Weiser, LLC
With offices at:
65 Parker Street, Suite 7
Newburyport, MA 01950
www.redwheelweiser.com
www.careerpress.com

ISBN: 978-1-60163-212-8

Library of Congress Cataloging-in-Publication Data
Smith, Jim, Jr.
    The no excuse guide to success : no matter what your boss-or life-
  throws at you / by Jim "Mr. Energy" Smith, Jr.
        p. cm.
    Includes index.
    ISBN 978-1-60163-212-8 -- ISBN 978-1-60163-603-4 (ebook)
      1. Motivation (Psychology) 2. Excuses--Psychological aspects.
    3. Success. 4. Success in business. 5. Self-actualization (Psychology)
    I. Title.

  BF503.S543 2012
  650.1--dc23

                                                      2012009705

Cover design by Ty Nowicki

Printed in the United States of America
IBI
10  9  8  7  6  5  4  3  2  1

This book is dedicated to my late great-grandmother Carrie Bryant, and my late grandmother Mary Lee Faulks. Your lessons and ongoing demonstrations of joy, love, and forgiveness continue to live with me today. You lived lives of giving, always making the person you were talking to feel as though he or she was the most important person in the world at that moment. I miss you both!

# Acknowledgments

A very special thank-you is extended to my awesome family: Gina (my wife—"God continues to bless us immensely"), Lauren, Daecia, Jordan, and Ian. Mom (R. Nanci Smith), Rodney, Michelle, Donavon, Joshua, Darin, Cheryl, Mom Williams, and Uncle Roy—I would not have been able to complete this project if you hadn't provided so much support and understanding during all of my mood shifts. Thank you for talking me off the cliff when I kept saying, "I'm never going to write another book during the Christmas holidays again." I love you!

A *big* high five and hug go out to my friend and editor (and voice of reason), Mark Morrow. If Superman wore an S on his chest, then I'd say you wear an S(plus). Thank you for your tireless support and understanding, and for pushing me to keep raising the bar on my writing. You brought out the best in me. This book did not get completed without you! You're amazing!

My appreciation also goes out to the JIMPACT team: Rodney Smith, Dr. Marie Amey-Taylor, Nancy Appleman-Vassil, James Charney, Laura Putnam, Michael Thompson, Ames Friedman Peinovich, Allison Manswell, Sandra Ann Dufault, and Marena Ariffin.

Rev. Dr. Kevin R. Johnson, Rev. Dr. George Taylor, Rev. Carmen Marshall, and Reverend Omari Hughes—thank you for all of your ongoing spiritual guidance and direction.

I'd like to thank the members of the Rutgers International Executive MBA Class of 2011. You were the ones who planted the seed that I needed to write a book on personal responsibility and accountability. Like I said during class, I think you gave me more than I gave you. I wish you continued success, peace, and joy. Thank you: Fionnie Wu, Carolyn Devanayagam, Ashley Brinson, Jenny Watson, Mary Beth Brinson, Michel Overstreet, Frank Stotzem, Doris Cao, Anthony Lee, Alexandra Tan, Antonio Pelicano, Brendon Gildea, Bruce Ni, Bruno deArruda, Elaine Zhu, Eugene Rosamilia, Fion Wei, Gopal Balasubramaniam, Horst Wahl, Jairo Escobar Ortega, Jeffrey Ouyang, Jessie Cheing, Jingwei Liu, Joseph Zhang, Kevin Ko, Kristin Glavitsch, Lawrence Nutting, Mandy Fan, Martin Wagner, Michael Chen, Ming Wu, Nelson Zhao, Radek Domagalski, Ram Weingarten, Zuojun Fang, Wayne Wang, Stefan Heinrich, Sharon Song, Santosh Kharti, and Roy Tan.

Thank you to my mentors, coaches, and confidants who helped to develop this book and keep me on track, including: Raimond and Bionda Honig, Reggie Hines, Mike Jones, Dr. R. Palan, Diana Nicholson, Annie Hart, Trish Uhl, Beth Rutter, Karen Cheng, Sardek Love, Dr. Marie Amey-Taylor, Kathy Dempsey, Isaac Collins, Claudia M. Shelton, Ken Frieson, Jim Brown, Uneeka Jay, Kelly Williams, Lauren Leonard, Renee Mack, P.J. Braam, B. Stern, J.D. Barker, Della Clark, Judy Chapman, Barry Callender, Anthony Spann, Ken and Lynn Shareef, Von Jordan, Lynae Remondino, Dolores Davis, Theresa Hummel-Krallinger, Grace Rudd, Sha Batt, Suran Casselle, Ruth Beedle, Sharon Furbur, Kathy Cook, Uva Coles, Dawn Ridenhour, Loraine Ballard Morrill, Kacey Jones, Crystal Reilly, Leslie Shields,

Skip and Rae Prince, Maria Garaitonandia, Griff and Meena Barger, Agata Szyler-Seidl, Bjorn Arild Wisth, Tonya Murphy, Yolanda Rocio, Deidre Graham-Childs, Dawn Mahoney, Janet Kloser, Farrokh Langdana, Mike Robinson, David Dec, Christina Joyce-Wilson, Sarita Lyons, Wendy Wolf, Lakshmi Pamidimukkala, Peter Renzulli, Sharon Rose, Laurie Adashek, and Toni Hendrix.

Finally, to my family, Titans, friends, colleagues, customers, supporters, and session participants (all over the world)—thank you for continuously challenging me, supporting me, encouraging me, and lifting me. You all make my heart smile.

# Contents

# Foreword

*Although I may be paralyzed physically, my dreams are not! Dreams become paralyzed only by personal belief.... Not by any tangible thing. They are unique! Dreams are created and attained by what we possess inside.*

—Chad Hymas

This is a masterfully written book that helps us to understand why it is time to stop making excuses—to own your own choices and to focus on the positive.

Jim shares examples of how to develop presentation skills, perfect leadership skills and finally discover your own personal power.

Learning through direct experiences of others solidifies our strengths and renders us the power to lead and live with enthusiasm, power, and purpose.

Not only has he witnessed those amazing "aha" moments, but, on one particular trip, he himself is provided a life-changing "aha" moment.

Jim tells the story of how he was impressed with a particular presentation from one of his students and what an impact it made on his life. Her example and story not only inspired others in the classroom to do better, but raised the bar for him as well!

This book inspires us all to make the choice of accepting complete and full responsibility, accountability, and credit for results achieved as a result of our actions. Moreover, when success finally comes, accept without apology or embarrassment your own accomplishments with the pride that comes along with doing something well.

For many, making excuses has been ingrained so much within us, that it has rendered us a bunch of pitiful, excuse-ridden creatures. He reminds us that if we are going to rid ourselves of this behavior, that it will take work—patience, perseverance and consistent practice—in order to make a positive change.

Jim takes us through the steps necessary for whatever you want to do—whether it is finding a better job, getting in shape, or searching for a new life partner. He offers help for those who are defensive, moody, and controlling—knowing that if you can change these features, you will find your inner peace.

Ten amazing principles are offered to reach that final positive outcome. Accountability is discussed in detail, as well as ownership of the choices we have made. He teaches us that if we live with purpose and urgency, our dreams await us.

One of the book's most profound quotes, given to Jim by his mentor Mike Jones, is as follows:

Life is not what you've been taught; it's what you believe. It's not what you've experienced; it's the choices you've made as a result. It's not about what happened to you, it's about how you've remembered it. It's not what challenges have come your way; it's what you've seen as challenging. It's not what has appeared on your path, it is what you have accepted. When we accept personal responsibility for our lives, everything is possible.

We are shown how to change our mental channel so that we may root out negative thoughts and we are taught the invaluable "5 Rs": which are Refocus, Revisit, Read, Resist, and Review.

Following the plan that Jim has brilliantly presented will indeed help you to "Do What Needs to Be Done" in order to reach your dreams.

—Chad Hymas CSP, CPAE

2011 Speaker Hall of Fame, internationally recognized author and speaker, the *Wall Street Journal*'s "One of the 10 Most Inspirational People," and world-record quadriplegic marathon and world-class athlete

*www.chadhymas.com*

# Preface

My trip to Shanghai, China, in May 2011 to teach a course on executive leadership for Rutgers University, began just like the two previous trips with lots of detailed planning and endless checklists.

- Prep class materials.
  - Syllabus, readings, articles, and the like (check).
  - Double-check technology (chargers, laptop, power cords, software updates, zip drives, etc.) (check).
  - Review Chinese Visa and make sure it's current (check).
- Pack for trip (Note: it's a 12-day trip with two 14-hour flights) (check).
- Schedule final JIMPACT team meeting (check).
- Look at final to-do list (check).
  - Urgent....
  - Follow up with....
  - Call....

Of course, someplace on the checklist are always the nonbusiness reminders to bring home gifts and presents for certain family members and friends as well as some very specific requests—for example, handbags for Gina (my wife), polo shirts and jewelry for Daecia (my 16-year-old daughter), and souvenirs and clothing for everyone else.

As I had done on my previous visits, I took a direct flight from Newark, New Jersey, to Shanghai. I cleared customs, retrieved my luggage without incident, and did my best to squeeze through the jam-packed throng of people crowded outside the exit gates waiting to welcome home family, friends, spouses, and soul mates. There was the typical cacophony of languages—from Chinese to Arabic—echoing around the gate area along with the strobe light effect created by a hundred flashing cameras trained on each hometown traveler as they emerged through the gate. I felt like a movie star facing down a pack of zealous paparazzi photographers.

I knew my Rutgers University driver would be standing somewhere nearby competing with a lot of other placard-waving drivers anxiously attempting to make eye contact with their assigned riders. The driver (his name was Bruce Zhang) and I made our connection without a hitch, and we headed back toward the city accompanied by an "old school" CD—Michael Jackson's *Greatest Hits*—blasting from the car's sound system. Yes!

The course I teach for the Rutgers University International Executive MBA (IEMBA) program is called "High Impact Executive Presentation Skills, Internal Leadership and Personal Power: A Potent Combination for Today's New Global Leader." The class usually draws an assortment of students from around the world, and I look forward to interacting with the diversity of cultures and languages. On this trip I had 39 students from China, Poland, Portugal, Germany, South America, Canada, Malaysia, Australia, South Africa, Israel, Singapore, Taiwan, India, Nepal, and the United States. I knew, based on past experience, that the students would show some initial hesitation to explore the world of people skills, but would soon be highly engaged with the class and would work diligently through the three key topics taught in the course:

- How to develop high impact executive presentation skills.

- How to perfect inside-out (managing from the heart) leadership skills.

- How to discover your own personal power.

By design, the classes deliberately shove students into their discomfort zones, especially the fear and loathing zones associated with making presentations. In fact, about 50 percent of each student's grade is determined by how well he or she makes presentations, leads group work, and participates and involves him- or herself in class discussions and projects. The point of the class is to not merely pass an exam or test, but to learn how to connect with, and inspire, people at many levels through direct experience that will internalize and solidify the strengths needed to lead and live with enthusiasm, power, and purpose.

In the four years I had been teaching this class I had seen many students experience profound "aha" moments. Some were even quite dramatic and moving, especially when they packed up and moved out of their "analytic zone," but this trip produced an experience that was a big, life-changing "aha" moment for me as well—so memorable, in fact, it deserves relating here.

## Alex's Story

From the first day in class, I could tell that Alexandra (Yayi/Alex), a Chinese student, was a lot more comfortable taking detailed notes than participating in any other class activity. She did fine with small breakout groups, but when she faced the riskier prospect of making a presentation to the entire group, I could tell she would rather have had root canal work.

Still, as I continued to observe her over the next three or four days in class, Alex seemed to be methodically building her courage and honing the technical details of public speaking. Then one day she just decided she was ready for prime time and was prepared to show us what she had learned.

I am a high-energy, walk-around presenter. I like to get up close and personal with my participants and model what I teach about effective presentations. So, with wireless microphone in hand, I typically cruise my audience and engage them directly. Alex's class had reached the point in the curriculum that required each participant to make a five-minute presentation. So when I asked if anyone in the class was prepared to make a presentation, I was surprised to see Alex's hand and body rising from the chair at the same time as she motioned for me to give her the microphone I was holding.

Alex didn't waste any time when she had the floor. She immediately launched into a rousing, well-prepared presentation on the assigned topic, which was to discuss the best leadership presentation *they* have ever heard or made themselves.

Alex was amazing—astounding even. She used appropriate gestures, paused dramatically, and practiced engaging voice inflection; she made eye communication with the audience and, surprisingly, she was even witty. Alex closed her presentation with a heartfelt, poignant call-to-action from the center of the room (a technique that I had taught her) and nailed it so well that she got a thunderous standing ovation from the other students.

During the next class break Alex approached me. I raised my hand to give her a high five. She smiled broadly when her hand met mine. Then she said to me, "Professor, I always talk myself out of speaking in public. I wanted to speak all week but I was afraid. Then yesterday, when the class expressed an interest in hearing more stories from Chinese students, I just decided that I was going to tell my story today despite all my fear."

Alex didn't know it, but her story had a big impact on me. In fact, her story of transformation is central to the themes presented in this book. Moreover, Alex's story, and the transformational stories from others in this special group of students, is one of the major reasons I wrote this book. I was impressed with Alex as much for the path she took, as for the path she did not take.

Alex could have made a lot of excuses to put off stepping up to the plate and facing her fears. She could have conjured up dozens of excuses with little thought or effort (my throat is sore today; I have a headache; I just need one more day to prepare; tomorrow I will absolutely do it).

Instead, Alex chose to do what is truly remarkable for many people: take action. Though the class learned only a few details about the specifics of Alex's life before she arrived in the classroom that day, we were privy to enough details in her short presentation to draw important conclusions about what her life was like before her breakthrough presentation, and what it would be like after her presentation.

Despite the significant restraints imposed by her own personal and family history as well as by her cultural and educational history, Alex got up that day and worked our classroom like a seasoned National Speakers Association, Dale Carnegie, or even Toastmaster speaker. Her powerful presentation caused a lot of the students (and even me) to tear up and boisterously chant "Alex! Alex! Alex!" She set the standard for her class and, from that day until the end of the class, she, and the rest of the students, continued to raise the success bar higher!

Alex made an important choice that day for herself and her future: She made a choice to reject her past history and to change what she expected would result from her actions. She decided to turn away from an expectation of failure to an expectation of competency and success as a public speaker. Alex also made a choice that day to do something that many of us fear beyond all else: the choice to take full responsibility, accountability, and credit for the results we achieve as a result of our actions. Remarkably, Alex learned that day to *expect* future success and then, when success came her way, accept it without apology or embarrassment. I know Alex will really "own" all her future accomplishments and really feel the pride that comes along with doing something well.

So welcome to a different path. Alex has blazed the trail for you so you have nothing to fear. Besides, if you're reading this book, then you probably know where the excuse road leads. So read on and remember this: Changing your life is a choice you make—so choose wisely, my friend.

—Jim "Mr. Energy" Smith, Jr.
February 2012

# Introduction

## No More Excuses!

I am not breaking any new ground here if I tell you right up front that most of us are absolutely addicted to making excuses. It's like a second career for us—avoiding responsibility and culpability for nearly everything that happens to us in life. We just can't seem to help ourselves.

In fact, excuse making is such an ingrained part of the human experience that many less excuse-prone people have taken time out from their busy careers doing things such as reinventing agricultural practice, discovering electricity, introducing social reform in healthcare and nursing, and creating timeless world literature, to let the rest of us know that many of us are, in fact, a bunch of pitiful, sad, excuse-ridden creatures. Here are a few examples:

- "Ninety-nine percent of the failures come from people who have the habit of making excuses." —George Washington Carver, scientist and researcher who developed alternative crops to cotton (peanuts, soybeans, and sweet potatoes)[1]

- "He that is good for making excuses is seldom good for anything else." —Benjamin Franklin, inventor, scientist, and statesman[2]

- "I attribute my success to this—I never gave or took any excuse."—Florence Nightingale, nurse, philosopher, statistician, and social reformer[3]
- "And oftentimes excusing of a fault doth make the fault the worse by the excuse." —William Shakespeare, *King John*[4]

So you'd think with such overwhelming evidence that excuse making holds so little water among those who actually get off their behinds and make something happen that we'd all just shut up and get busy!

But, unfortunately, getting rid of the excuse habit is like getting rid of any other addiction; it takes work, sweat, patience, perseverance, and consistent practice in order to make positive change. Sorry, but there's no easy road to take here. If you're not willing to face the music and really work the principles outlined in this book, I'm afraid reading this book might just end up feeding right into your excuse addiction. If you're already leaning in the excuse direction, I'll make it easy for you. You can use this reasonable excuse right now and save yourself some time. Repeat after me:

*"Well, I really do want to develop a healthier, more positive attitude and I thought this book was going to help me. Unfortunately, I just don't have the time to practice the techniques the book advises. This is a busy time in my life. Why do I have to write stuff down, anyway? Isn't reading enough? But I do plan to try again later when things slow down a little and when I can focus more energy and time on this. I know it's important, but for now...."*

## Just the Annoying Facts

So, we've established pretty clearly that excuse making is as common as driving while talking on your cell phone and that few of us are immune from its comfortable appeal. But, here's another annoying—but perfectly understandable—aspect about facing up to our undeniable track record of excuse making (or any other destructive habit we might have developed over the years). Wait for it...you know what it is... we *really, really, really, really, realllly* HATE it when someone calls us out on it. Ouch!

If you need an all-too-familiar example, try suggesting a different course of action other than excuses the next time your teenage daughter or son whines about why it's impossible to improve a U.S. history, Latin, or math grade. Except for a few impossibly mature teenagers out there (you know, the ones you point to as positive examples when having this "take responsibility" conversation with your children), you know that getting most teenagers to listen to an alternative approach is like watching Chris Rock without laughing. It's just not going to happen. If you do try, your conversations will go something "like" those that follow no matter how much leverage or expertise you have to offer:

You: "Hey, did you know that your father took Latin when he was in school? I can help you get your grade up."

Teen: "That's okay. I'll get it eventually. I don't really know why they're making us take this class. I'm never, like, going to have to speak in Latin! It's a stupid dead language that is not even related to English!"

OR

You: "Wow! This is great! I just learned that your class is using the U.S. history book that I happen to have written. Why didn't you tell me?"

Teen: "You can't help me. That wouldn't be fair, and besides, we just Google everything anyway. We just use your book, like, for reference. I'll be all right."

OR

You: "You don't understand math? I can help. I told you math was my favorite subject in school and, after all, I use math all day long in my work. This will give us an opportunity to spend some quality time together."

Teen: "Please, Mom. Math has changed, like, a lot since you were in school. I'll just go over to P.J.'s house to study. She has a math video game that's really cool!"

As you see, no excuse bar is high enough, no matter what you're offering. If your teen, or anyone else for that matter, is committed to excuse making, that's the way it will be until a choice is made to change.

## The Big Change

Of course, teenagers are a whole different class of humans, and thankfully they become responsible as they grow up. In most cases, teenage negativism dissipates as the brain matures, but at some level we all have moments when we'd like to return to the good old days when weaseling out of responsibility was so easy to do. Unfortunately, that was then. This is now!

So if you are ready to do the work needed, and to face the embarrassment and perhaps pain of staring down your fears, then this book will definitely help you. I promise that you will find a sympathetic ear in the pages that follow, but I won't promise that I'll be the friend, colleague, spouse, or stranger waiting in a grocery store line listening and perhaps agreeing with all your excuses.

What I promise instead is to be your coach and mentor. I am absolutely dedicated to helping you take all the necessary steps to change or improve your situation. So, what do you really want to do? No matter what action you want to take, I am here to help you if you've really decided it's time to take action. If you want to:

- Change jobs but have dithered around unable to take even the smallest steps toward that goal— I'm here to provide the push.

- Start your own company but are afraid to give up your P&B (paycheck and benefits)—I've got the motivational words for you.

- Get in shape, or find a new or improved life partner— you can count on me for help.

- Take time for a vacation, write a book, get another degree, or learn general accounting principles (okay, even I can find excuses for this one!)—I'm down for that.

- Stop being the defensive, moody, miserable, controlling, and insecure person you know deep down that you are—I'm on your change team.

- Stop insisting that others change first to suit your vision of the world—I'm your voice of reason.

- Find your inner joy and peace—yes, I can help with that, too.

This book, and the principles it offers, will help you obtain these goals and much more.

## What I Can't Fix

The one thing I absolutely will *not* help you do is continue on the path of becoming just another serial excuse maker (SEM), someone who believes that success (and happiness) waits just beyond the day you get past your current circumstance ("As soon as I get this...or do that...or finish... something") and then you promise yourself that you'll work toward the life you want.

We all know this way of thinking is tired and that change has always been the rub. I believe this book can be a powerful ally if you truly want to leave excuses behind and forge ahead with a new and better path. If you are able to fully commit to living the principles I offer in this book and use the practical tools I offer, then I am completely confident that you'll achieve at least the following positive outcomes. You'll be able to:

- Make life-altering changes in how you approach your career and your life.
- Stop blaming others and start believing in yourself.
- Own your choices and break down self-created barriers to success.
- Embrace uncertainty and stop being afraid to win.

I know from firsthand experience how debilitating and depressing it is to be caught in a cycle of excuses, and I know that the path out of an excuse-making habit is not easy to follow, nor is it quickly accomplished. You see, I too was "somewhat" of a serial excuse maker until I decided—really decided—it was time to stop. The transition for me was made easier because I had great spiritual and professional mentoring and the strong support of friends and family.

It's your turn now. I want to be your fully committed, encouraging, supporting personal guide and mentor for your change journey. I promise that if you stick with me you'll find, as I did, that it's a journey worth taking.

## About This Book

This book offers my 10 proven principles (Winning Ways) that will help you move beyond making excuses and toward living the life you want. These principles—personal power, personal responsibility, positive attitude, and taking action—are the same principles that have engaged and motivated the thousands who have attended my workshops, seminars, and keynote addresses. Whether I'm speaking in China, Malaysia, Europe, the Bahamas, or the United States, just the idea that "we" (you and I personally) have the power to radically change the direction and outcome of our lives never fails to resonate with my audiences. The joyful, often tear-filled "aha" moments when those in my audience realize that radical, life-altering change is possible and that a better, more fulfilling future is possible, are always the same no matter the language they speak, their cultural norms, or their social status. It is rewarding work, indeed!

So, here's a brief snapshot of the chapters in this book and the principles taught in each. Reading the descriptions should be an exciting preamble to the work you're just about to begin.

### Introduction: No More Excuses

The gauntlet is thrown. Are you up to the challenge of a no excuse life?

## Winning Way 1: Own Your Choices

Accountability is the focus of this chapter. It's all about owning your choices and decisions. It's about owning your role in whatever happens to you. We *chose* to stay in unhappy situations. We *chose* to deceive our employers about our job satisfaction. We *chose* to put off studying for a final exam until the last minute. We *chose* to spend our money erratically. We *chose* to avoid taking risks.

You will be challenged to change perspectives and avoid the use of the term *mistake* for anything you might have control over. You will be pushed to internalize the basic truth that most of the decisions we make (yes or no, positive or negative) are conscious choices. You have much more power than you believe you have over the final outcome. You will be encouraged to own your "stuff" as the first step in a process that builds a sustainable cycle of responsibility and empowers you to achieve your desired goals.

## Winning Way 2: Focus on Positive Outcomes and Expect Success

Focusing on the problem is easy. Finding fault and blame is easy. Finding solutions? Now, that is difficult work! It is easy—perhaps a natural tendency—to clearly see the obstacles to success and to minimize the possibility for a successful outcome. I'll introduce the concept of "what you think about, you will be about." Yes, it is positive thinking psychology, but you need a way to get there. This chapter will show you a better way to travel by focusing on the vision first. You'll be surprised how quickly the "how" part reveals itself once you trust that a solution is possible. I'll give you some practical and well-tested tools to help you keep your focus on a positive or successful outcome, including some tips on defeating unproductive "distraction-thinking."

### Winning Way 3: Embrace the Uncertainty

Successful, positive people "lean into their discomfort" and "feel the fear and do it anyway." You will be challenged to move out of your safety zone and to avoid "comfort-zone thinking." For my money, singer/songwriter Tim McGraw's 2004 hit, "Live Like You Were Dying," from the album of the same name, just about says it all. I will show you in this chapter how to move beyond living life in "neutral" and how to "put yourself out there" despite the imagined and frightening consequences.

### Winning Way 4: Do More With Your Best

Corporations and businesses often rethink their business models in order to find innovative new ways of doing business. You should take a page from the corporate playbook and reinvent, reconfigure, and reset your own familiar internal processes and methodologies for solving problems and facing the challenges of life. In this chapter, I will push you to *stop* searching for answers to problems "out there." Instead, I'll show you why in most cases the answers to your toughest problems are very likely right in front of you, just waiting to be recognized and used. You can start by taking a long, hard look at the face staring back at you each morning in the bathroom mirror. As someone once told me, "You can't escape yourself. After all, you take you with you everywhere you go."

### Winning Way 5: Listen With Three Ears

Our disengaged listening habits are directly linked to the fast-paced, get-it-done-now world we all inhabit, and I argue that this disengagement is part of the excuse-making habit. In this chapter you'll learn how to listen and interact with others in ways that increase the quality and effectiveness of your communication. Many of the techniques I offer are simple, but their impact can a have powerful impact on how you're able to take charge of the world around you: avoid multitasking while listening, and refrain from judging and formulating responses when listening, for example. Finally, I ask you to examine all the cultural and personal history differences among us and to examine how this "baggage" interferes with honest and effective exchange.

## Winning Way 6: Remove Self-Created Barriers

Self-created barriers take away our power to take positive action. You'll examine how to bring down these walls and thoughts about why they were built in the first place—to protect us from pain, disappointment, and rejection. I'll show you why the serial excuse maker's greatest fear is not fear of failure, but the even more frightening prospect of the fear of success! Whether you are considering starting your own company, returning to school, or pursuing a romantic interest, you'll learn why these self-created roadblocks are often the most difficult barriers to overcome.

## Winning Way 7: Pursue Your Passion, Not a Paycheck

Employers understand the power of an engaged workforce. Employees with the right skills and a passion for what they do are in high demand. Yet, most of us don't have a clear connection to, or understanding of, our workplace passion. Yes, the admonition of "just do what you love and success will follow" still applies, but many of us are still searching for what "it" might be. In this chapter I'll show you how to truly engage with your work and ultimately your life. You will find practical tools to help you discover the "one thing" that you are most passionate about, along with ways to ensure that you make pursuing this passion a way of life.

## Winning Way 8: Give Up "Right-Fighting"

Wouldn't it be great if we were never wrong? What if everyone agreed with us no matter what we said? This chapter is about the all too human tendency I call the "yes, but..." cycle. I will show you how to break the "yes, but..." cycle and why this response to any challenge to your established "fact," or way of thinking, or strongly held opinion, rarely leads to understanding; it certainly does not lead to the formation of common purpose. Moreover, it's just one more way we can avoid positive change (aka excuse making). As personal power expert Les Brown puts it, "but is an argument for your limitations and when you argue for your limitations you get to keep them."[5] You will learn to actively listen, seek common connection and purpose, and find win-win solutions through dialogue and positive negotiation techniques.

## Winning Way 9: Avoid the "Taking Credit" Trap

Basketball great John Wooden once said, "It is amazing how much can be accomplished if no one cares who gets the credit."[6] This chapter focuses on selflessness and giving. I'll show you why developing an attitude of *contribution*, not *attribution*, often leads to surprising results both in the workplace and at home and how, once you "get" this concept, you'll see your excuse-making tendencies drop dramatically. The chapter also offers exercises and checklists that you can use to evaluate your own self-aggrandizement quotient. You'll also learn how to balance a healthy amount of self-promotion with a reasonable amount of "credit taking."

## Winning Way 10: Live With Urgency and Purpose

If you've made it this far in the book and taken to heart what you've learned up until now, then I should be able let you in on a little news flash: There's no excuse for you to keep your dreams and goals in the "waiting room of life." You should be able to emerge from behind the self-imposed shields that hide your insecurities and fears so that you are able to engage *fully* with life! I'll show you how to be constantly working on your TAN (take action now) so that you'll always be living a life that is "all in" and excuse-free. At the end of the chapter, you'll be able to complete an action plan exercise designed to get you immediately started on your Urgency and Purpose TAN quotient. If you do well enough, you'll be awarded the status of No Excuse Master, and you'll get a certificate to "go and make excuses no more." You'll be surprised what his certification will buy you in your career and life!

Welcome to the first day of the best days of your life! Good luck!

## How to Use This Book

This book is designed to be an interactive tool that will help you take action on the principles I outline to lead a No Excuse Life. To that end, I encourage you to interact with the book and use the prompts provided to make notes, consider challenges, and think through situations in order to jot down positive next steps.

### Stop, Start, Continue Icons

At the end of each chapter you'll see three Icons—STOP, START, and CONTINUE—associated with next step options to help you on your no excuse journey. These icons are designed to graphically get you moving in a positive direction and to stop making excuses for why today is "not a good day" to make these needed changes in your life.

## No Excuses Online

To help you continue to live a no excuse life, I have developed a no excuse Website (*www.noexcuseguide.com*). The Website houses a number of the exercises, application forms, and reminders from the book. Please visit the Website to access and print these forms, and while you're there, please share your comments regarding how successful you've been in eliminating your excuses.

## Pre-Test

In many educational settings, a pre-test is often given to assess the knowledge students have on a particular topic before formal instruction begins. The scores of the individual students are then used as a baseline to determine the learning progress in the class.

So, think of this as your no excuse pre-test. If you fully engage with the ideas in this book, you will be surprised at the progress you've made by the time you finish the last chapter of this book.

### —No Excuses Pre-Test—

First, here are some typical and familiar excuses:

- I just don't have the time or the energy right now.
- It will work out eventually.
- It's out of my control now.
- There are no other jobs out there.

And, here are some good reasons to *not* make excuses:

- I have to take control of my life!
- I created this mess. Now I'm going to clean it up!
- I see now that I can use some help!
- I going to take action now!

**At the end of this book, I will:**

Stop

1. _____
   _____

2. _____
   _____

3. _____
   _____

4. _____
   _____

5. _____
   _____

Start

1. _____
   _____

2. _____
   _____

3. _____
   _____

4. _____
_____

5. _____
_____

Continue

1. _____
_____

2. _____
_____

3. _____
_____

4. _____
_____

5. _____
_____

## Goals and Outcome Sharing

One of the best ways to build support for the changes you wish to make in your life is through the use of social networking. Throughout this book, you'll be encouraged to share your learning with your network of colleagues, friends, and family through the use of Facebook, Twitter, and other social network applications.

The first exercise is a "future state" sharing that we'll just call your pre-share test. Here's the prompt:

Imagine that you have finished the book and you've been completely successful at changing your excuse-making habit. You've fully implemented the 10 Winning Ways covered in this book, and you're happier and more confident than you've been in years.

Now, sit with that for a moment and then imagine that you're ready to share this new way of approaching the world with your social network. What would you want to say to your social network that would introduce your personal community to the "new you"?

Jot down your imagined post in the space provided.

# Winning Way 1

## Own Your Choices

*People say to me, you were a roaring success.
How did you do it? I go back to what my parents
taught me. Apply yourself. Get all the education you can,
but then, by God, do something. Don't just stand there;
make something happen.*
—Lee Iacocca, president and CEO, Chrysler[1]

The first principle of this book is so important that I'm going to let you in on a little secret right up front: If this principle describes your approach to life, then you don't need my book. If you are someone who already takes responsibility for the choices you make and the consequences that may follow, then you are clearly *not* a member of the Whine Club. You won't find much in the following pages you don't already know and practice. For everyone else, stick around to learn how you can catch up. Here's what you'll learn to get you back on track:

- Why we enjoy blaming others so much.
- The difference between mistakes and choices.
- The 10 stops and starts of owning your choices.
- How you can move from being a Whiner in Denial to a Winner in Demand.

## Breaking the Whining Habit

Maybe you think that breaking the whining habit should be easy enough to do—certainly no more difficult than jettisoning other counterproductive, life-limiting behaviors from your life. You simply make up your mind to change and—voilá!—the next time a whining opportunity presents itself, you'll change course like a train switching its tracks, and head in a new and more productive direction.

Once you've accepted the rapid-switch fantasy, then it's very easy to imagine the *new you* out there taking responsibility and owning the consequences of all your decisions. "From this day forward," you say to yourself after you've internalized this new, liberating, life-changing epiphany, "I will no longer blame others, and I *will* take full responsibility for all my actions. When I mess up I will *absolutely* accept both the blame and consequences of my actions!"

You feel lightheaded and giddy as you imagine your world up to now and then envision your new world *from this moment on*! In fact, you may feel so good about your decision that you call your best friend to share the news.

"What's up, BFF?" you say with excitement in your voice. "I've got awesome news!"

"Oh, really? Tell me!" your friend says.

"You know that annoying tendency I have always had to never take responsibility for absolutely anything—you know, the habit that you say just drives you *nuts*?"

"Yes."

"Well, it's gone! Kaput! Not happening anymore. I'm done with that. From now on 'personal responsibility' will be my middle name! From now on, I'm going to be known as a doer, not a whiner. What do you think?

[Silence.]

"Hey, buddy? You there?"

"Yes," your friend says. "Sorry, I was just noting this day on my calendar so that I can remind you of this conversation the next time you tell me that your boss is a half-wit who ignores all your ideas."

## The Natural State of Blame

Blaming comes so naturally to us it's almost a knee-jerk reaction. Someone stops speaking to you for a minor misunderstanding—it's their problem, not yours. You get fired from your job—it's your manager's fault because he didn't appreciate your contributions. Your business or sales team loses customers or key clients—it's the economy's fault. You and your spouse or significant other don't get along—it's his or her fault.

Although it's true that friends are sometimes unreasonable, bosses are often unfair, the world economy can be cruel and heartless, or those closest to you may be in need of some one-on-one time with Dr. Phil, at the end of the day the only pertinent question worth asking is this: "What am I going to do about it?" Like my mom always said, "Life's not fair. Get used to it and get over it."

Here's a recent example of the blame game in action. I recently called the lost and found department of a car rental company to inform them that I had left my Day-Timer and laptop power cord in the car I had recently rented. After waiting on hold for close to 10 minutes, the sales agent who finally picked up the phone apologized and promised a return call within 20 minutes. Of course, I got no follow-up call, so I proactively called again, and got the same "we'll call you back in 20 minutes" answer. On my third call back to the car rental agency, I was promised an "end of the day" return call.

Finally, two days and several more phone calls (one with a manager) later, I talked with the same sale representative who had not called me back initially. She offered to help, but first blamed the company and her boss for not staffing the front desk properly during busy, peak times of the day. She never said she was sorry for my inconvenience or frustration. That was her story, and she was sticking to it.

## My Own Blame Game Story

I shake my head in dismay when I think about my early years in the corporate setting. Believe it or not, I learned to play the blame game very well. I began to look to others as the root cause of negative outcomes or failures. It was a predictable routine: I'd spend time thinking the situation through, clearly considering my role in the outcome. Once I was sure that I'd left no stone unturned as to my own culpability, the finger-pointing and denial began. I didn't own my stuff, and I made excuses. It was *my* story, and I stuck to it!

We all know at some level that this blame game behavior is a road to nowhere. But like a lot of others who have made a radical shift in their approach to life or experienced a profound attitude change, it took a singularly awful and painful experience to convince me that I needed to take my life in a different direction.

Eighteen years ago I was a novice, but highly motivated management development training consultant for the Vanguard Group. Although I liked my job, what I really wanted to be was an internationally known motivational speaker and a successful professional development consultant and trainer. So when a seasoned motivational trainer (with a big reputation) showed up to conduct a one-day diversity-awareness session at my company, I took this as a sign from above that this was the right time to make my move.

I introduced myself, and within three months I was traveling around the country presenting my own brand of diversity training as a subcontract employee of the training firm known as Tim Golden and Associates; it didn't take long for Tim to become my mentor and trusted friend. One day a client who had taken a particular interest in my diversity training style and approach, confided that they were going to end Tim's training contract. I was asked to continue providing training as an independent contractor until a new training firm was found.

When I approached Tim about taking the offer from the client company after his contract was terminated, he got angry, even though I was an independent subcontractor and not technically his employee. In spite of his ire, I stayed on with the client and continued training. I reasoned that if he was doing a credible job they would not have ended the contract—at least, that's what they told me.

That decision ended a valued relationship and, instead of facing the possibility that my own ethical compass was askew, I shifted the blame away from me through rationalization and blame shifting. The truth is that I made a horrible *choice*, and it's a choice I regret to this day. I just couldn't admit that my friend was absolutely right.

For me, this incident was the beginning of a blame game metamorphosis. The incident made crystal clear for me the *huge* difference between choices and mistakes. I realized with shocking clarity that I had made an awful choice in the situation—not a mistake. I could have chosen a much better path, but I didn't. I now take responsibility for that choice.

# Choices and Mistakes: What's the Difference?

Andy Andrews nailed the difference between choices and mistakes with unrivaled clarity in his classic book, *The Noticer*.[2] I was simply captivated by the following description. Andrews writes:

> If one makes a mistake, then an apology is usually sufficient to get things back on an even keel. However—and this is a big *however*—most people do not ever know why their apology did not seem to have any effect. It is simply that they did not make a mistake; they made a choice...and never understood the difference between the two.
>
> ...If you are lost, wandering through a forest in the dark, unable to see, unaware that a cliff is nearby, and you stumble off the cliff and break your neck that is a mistake.... But let's say it's broad daylight. You are meandering about in a forest you've been told never to enter. There are No Trespassing signs everywhere, but you think you can slip in and slip out and not get caught. Now, again let's say you fall off a cliff and break your neck...that, my friend, was not a mistake. It was a conscious choice.
>
> When one simply makes a mistake, an apology— an "I'm sorry"—will usually handle the situation. But when a choice has been identified, the only way to repair a relationship is by exhibiting true remorse and seeking forgiveness. Now in some cases, where money or property might have been involved, you should offer restitution, but showing real remorse and actually asking the question "Will you please forgive me?" is the only pathway to a new beginning in your business or personal life.

## The Big Reg Story

Here's another example of this important concept about the difference between choices and mistakes, and the power of taking responsibility for both.

I met Reggie Hines in 1979 during my freshman year at Widener University. Big Reg and I were members of the football team, and he was probably one of the best and most gifted athletes I ever knew. He was 6'4" and carried around 235 pounds of muscle that he could translate into bursts of amazing speed and gridiron agility. Whereas many freshmen were happy to just make the varsity team, Reg played and started every game at tight end his freshman season, winning several offensive awards for his efforts.

Unfortunately, Big Reg transferred from Widener after only one year and enrolled at West Chester University (Pennsylvania). He earned All-Conference honors and went on to set a number of school records over the next couple of years, earning tryouts with the Dallas Cowboys and other NFL teams. It was a time of great possibility for Big Reg. He was living his dream and the hopes and dreams of his entire family—always a big weight to carry.

Then the Cowboys and other teams took a pass on the opportunity to sign Big Reg to a long-term contract. This was a big disappointment to the normally positive, can-do athlete, and he wasn't equipped to handle it in the end.

He gave up his dreams and moved on with his life—or so he thought. He got married, and started a family and a successful family auto-detailing business. But his failure to make a life as a professional football player constantly nagged and taunted him. Like many others who've had big disappointments in life, Reg turned to drugs for relief, which led inevitably to the loss of everything he once valued, including his family.

After several near-death scrapes, Big Reg did eventually decide to take responsibility for his life and decisions, and charted a new path for his life. Here's what he told me about his transformational experience as we sat at the famed Palestra watching the University of Pennsylvania and Drexel University go at it for 40 spirited minutes on the basketball court:

> I blamed the Dallas Cowboys for not giving me a fair shot. I blamed the New York Giants for bringing me to camp and building up my hope after they had just won the Super Bowl with the two great tight ends they already had. I blamed my ex-wife for not being more understanding and supportive. I blamed my agent for not getting me more tryouts. I blamed everybody. But over the years I've had time to reflect on everything and I now realize it was my fault. I'm just blessed to still be living and to have the wonderful children, friends, and career that I have.

Big Reg's story is a great example of how owning your choices and outcomes is so liberating. He made a conscious choice to change his mindset and choose a different way of interacting with the world. He said he made changes across the board, from strengthening his religious faith, to his dress and choice of associates, to his physical health and his connection to, and involvement in, his community. As my own mentor and friend, Mike Jones routinely points out to me during our coaching calls:

> Life is not what you've been taught; it's what you believe. It's not what you've experienced; it's the choices you've made as a result. It's not about what happened to you, it's about how you've remembered it. It's not what challenges have come your way; it's what you've seen as challenging. It's not what has appeared on

*your path; it is what you have accepted. When we ac-
cept personal responsibility for our lives, everything
is possible.*

## 10 Stops and Starts to Owning Your Choices

So, how do you get started on owning your choices? It's
not really that hard. It's not rocket science or brain surgery
or even as hard as driving through a thunderstorm with bad
windshield wipers. You just have to decide to get started. But
be forewarned: If you want to own your choices and take
personal responsibility for your actions, you'll need to make
a significant mindset shift away from your old habits, especially if you want your new attitude to stick and become a
way of life. But it can be done.

The following are the steps I share with leaders, managers, individuals, and students around the world as I encourage them to embrace their personal power and to own their
choices. It's a message that crosses cultures and customs. It's
the first step in a process that sets in motion the cycle of taking responsibility that empowers and leads to the achievement of your goals in life. These 10 points are easy to read
and visualize accomplishing, and all it takes to accomplish
them are your personal dedication, strength of character,
and patience. So, what do you have to lose except your old
practices that are guaranteed to fail you?

## 10 Stops and Starts to Owning Your Choices

1. Stop being defensive when you're held accountable for your poor choices.

2. Stop being irritable and angry when you don't get your way.

3. Stop looking for what's wrong with the other person.

4. Stop being a victim.

5. Stop thinking negatively (and masking it by saying you're just keeping it real).

6. Start saying "I got this!" when the going gets tough.

7. Start asking for specific, clear feedback for improvement.

8. Start listening without judging.

9. Start focusing on the possibility and not the problem.

10. Start following through on your promises. Period.

## The Details

1.  **Stop being defensive when you're held account-able for your poor choices.** The next time your boss or manager confronts you with a mistake or poor choice you've made, don't start with a denial and put up an impenetrable defensive wall. If you keep doing this, you'll soon start to believe your excuses. Take time to focus on why you resort to this tactic. Embrace feedback. Consider it a gift. Learn from your choices and move on. Put down the boxing gloves. If someone is helping you with a character-building moment, just say, "Thank you," and make the necessary adjustments.

2.  **Stop becoming irritable and angry when you don't get your way.** I know people with a 0-to-60 temper that's faster than an Indianapolis 500 race car. You can see it in their eyes as all their energy and body language coalesce around the disappointment of not getting their way. I'm going to keep it real here: Grow up! Stop being selfish and self-centered. The world doesn't revolve around you! There are always two sides to every situation. Lean into your discomfort. Seek alternatives. Grow and learn from the no's. It's easy to get mad. It's what most people do. Winners are always looking for ways to grow, not just go through adversity.

3.  **Stop looking for what's wrong with the other person.** Come on. You can do it. Tilt the mirror your way. Even the late entertainer Michael Jackson has some advice for you here in the famous 1987 song "Man in the Mirror": "I'm looking at the man in the mirror; I'm asking him to

change his ways."[3] Until you accept the possibility that you may be wrong, you will be stuck permanently blaming others. Mike Jones, my mentor, hit the sweet spot when he explained to me that we all have maps created through our upbringing and experiences. Unfortunately, we get in trouble when we think our map should be standardized across all humanity. Simply look in before you look out to blame others; check for your own responsibility.

4. **Stop being a victim.** As a recovered victim, I know firsthand how easy it is to fall into this trap. Being a victim is easier than being responsible. You feel as though everyone is against you. It's never your fault. At a subconscious level, you begin to believe that you wear a bull's-eye target on your back and the world is constantly target practicing. Change the script. Change your approach. Change your mind-set. Move from victim to victor!

5. **Stop thinking negatively (and masking it by saying you're just keeping it real).** Negativity abounds in our society. It's more prevalent than green grass on a golf course. I'm amazed by the number of people in my life, both professionally and personally, who routinely think and respond in negative terms. Simply put, you are what you think, say, and do. What *you* focus on becomes *your* focus. It's not a hard concept to understand, but it's exceptionally hard to put into practice. Rod Hairston, in his inspirational book, *Are You Up for The Challenge?* says this about positive and negative thinking:

You will bring into your life whatever you consistently hold in your thoughts. The thoughts that you send out will show up in your life. When I ask people, "What do you really want?" most people start their answer with, "Well, I know what I don't want...." Or, they'll say, "I don't want to be exhausted," or "I don't want to be angry all the time." Unfortunately, that's how we've been trained our whole lives. We were taught to think about what we don't want, so this thinking becomes automatic. If you spend your time thinking about what you don't want, that's what you'll attract: more of what you don't want.[4]

What's hard about that concept? Once again, whether or not you follow through is your decision.

6. **Start saying "I got this!" when the going gets tough.** The best athletes thrive when the pressure is the greatest. Up to bat when the bases are loaded? No problem. Taking an overtime penalty shot when the division championship hangs in the balance? No worries. Professional athletes thrive on the exhilaration found on the other side of tough challenges—a 90-yard drive toward the end zone in the last 59 seconds of the game or a Hail Mary shot across the length of the basketball court that swooshes through the net as the buzzer sounds. Do these incredible scenarios always happen? Of course not, but the possibility of any other possibility playing out never crosses the mind of a seasoned athlete. From beginning

to end, these athletes take responsibility for the final outcome. They have an "accountability mind-set." Remember: Winners work to create the outcomes they want. Whiners just complain about the final score and pass the blame to someone else.

7. **Start asking for specific, clear feedback for improvement.** Feedback and coaching have played a significant role in my life. I live for and welcome it. It's absolutely true that seeing yourself as others see you is nearly impossible. Humans are not built for this sort of self-examination. You can't see the skyline if you're stuck in the traffic. Of course I'm not suggesting taking all feedback as the gospel truth. Not everyone has your best interests at heart. No surprise there. The trick is to use your Titans, mentors, and "true" friends to give you both praise (what you do well) and polish (what you should consider doing differently).

One of my Titans, Annie Hart, founder and owner of Breakthrough Coaching, Training and Storytelling, asked me during one of our coaching sessions if I ever get flustered or lose control of the room when I'm training or speaking. I answered, "No." She then asked me if I get flustered and lose control at home during heated discussions. I admitted I did. Then she asked me if I might use the same techniques and tools at home as I do when training or speaking. I felt like I just won the lottery. She helped me to see something I'd never considered before. I know it seems obvious, but, as noted, self-awareness is not one of our core competencies. Finally (and this is key), during your feedback moments, *listen* and don't interrupt, and make sure you understand the feedback. Here, the "I-know-what-you-think-I-said-but-that's-not-what-I-said" principle applies.

8. **Start listening without judging.** Do you listen to understand, or do you listen to criticize or find fault? Do you find yourself anxiously waiting for the other person to pause for a half-second so you can launch in with your own comments or pursue your own agenda? It's a good thing we're not given pop quizzes at the end of these one-sided conversations. One of the reasons people don't remember the feedback or instructions they're given is because their focus is to find fault with what the other person is saying. Or perhaps the person getting feedback is actively determining whether or not he should listen based on what he believes to be true. How often have you said, during a conversation, "That's not what I said"? We jump to judge! Stop being defensive. Stop right-fighting. You should ask the person you're having a conversation with whether or not she feels you're actively listening. Put down your judge's gavel and give new information a chance.

9. **Start focusing on the possibility and not the problem.** I alluded to this somewhat in Stop 5. Mike Jones, my mentor and empowerment expert, coined the acronym FOTO (focus on the outcome). We tend to focus on the distractions, the circumstances, the barriers, and the hurdles, and we give those factors way too much power and time. What you believe to be true generally turns out to be your reality. It really is standard "pop"

psychology, but nothing could be more dead-on accurate. If you believe you can start your own company and take your idea or talents to new levels, then you've taken the most important step. Belief must come before the *how* in order to make it happen. Whine Club members spend most of their time focusing on what might go wrong. You should focus on what you know *will* go right. As motivational guru and author Rod Hairston says:

> Focus on possibilities and on the compelling future you're working toward, instead of dwelling on doubts and on an imperfect past. Focus on growing and expanding instead of fearfully staying in your comfort zone. Focus on abundance instead of scarcity. Focus on what is right with your life instead of what's wrong. When you do that, you'll give energy to the things you want in your life, which will help manifest them.[5]

10. **Start following through on your promises. Period.** This final point requires some bullet points for emphasis:

- STOP trying. START doing.
- Keep everyone in the loop. Communicate.
- Just say "no" if you don't really believe your own promise.
- Know that any financial promise not fulfilled is *always* a bad idea.
- Base your follow-up promise on what *you* have control over.

You likely could add to these bullet points, but the point is clear: You do have some control over the promises you make and, given how most humans operate, people do not delete their "disappointment files." So, just take responsibility and get something done.

## Own Your Choices: A Winning Sustainability Plan

Now that you've got the basics down, it's time to put some action plans in place. The following exercise is designed to help you take that next step.

If the first step toward change is your realization that something has to change, the following exercise should help you take that first step. It's designed to let you make broad observations and commitments to change. We'll get to more specific techniques later in the book, but for now, getting something down on paper is the goal. If you'd rather do this digitally, go to *www.noexcuses.com* and jot down your answers there.

The following is a set of circumstances and choices that apply to most of us. You will find two prompts per situation or topic. One is an **Up to Now** prompt, and the other is a **From Now On** prompt. You should find doing this exercise not that stressful and it should condition you for the harder work that follows.

### —Stops and Starts Exercise—

Think about how you have conducted your own life up until now. If possible, you should do this contemplation when you are not rushed or distracted by anything else. So try not to do this exercise while watching reruns of *Saturday Night Live*, while listening to NPR, or during your commute on the train or bus. You really need to do some serious self-assessment for this activity to do you any good.

When you're ready, answer the following questions based on the 10 Stops and Starts of taking responsibility. Be honest. No one is watching or listening. If you can do this, then you've already made progress with taking responsibility for yourself. Be forewarned: You may be surprised (or even frightened) by what you learn about yourself. On the positive side, think of the exercise as a time machine; you now have a chance to rewrite history.

**Stop**  **Stop being defensive when someone holds you accountable for your poor choices.**

Think of a recent situation or circumstance when your poor choices resulted in someone holding you accountable. How did you react? Did you react in a defensive way? Here's your chance to rewrite history. First, describe your current way of dealing with these accountability situations (**Up to Now**). Then, jot down what you think would have been a better way to deal with the situation or circumstance (**From Now On**).

**Up to Now:** When I'm in a situation or a circumstance like this, I

_____

_____

_____

_____

_____.

**From Now On:** When I'm in this situation or circumstance I will

_____

_____

_____

_____ .

**Stop being irritable and angry when you don't get your way.**

Stop

Think of a situation or circumstance when you immediately went red-zone after you didn't get your way. Why did you blow up? Was it a situation you experienced before? Did you do all that you could to avoid the outcome? First, describe your current way of dealing with these accountability situations (**Up to Now**). Then, jot down what you think would have been a better way to deal with the situation or circumstance (**From Now On**).

**Up to Now:** When I'm in a situation or a circumstance like this I

_____

_____

_____

_____ .

**From Now On:** When I'm in this situation or circumstance I will

_____

_____

_____

_____ .

**Stop** Stop looking for what's wrong with the other person.

Think of a recent situation or circumstance when you totally focused on what the other person did rather than on your role in the circumstance or situation. How did you react? Did you react in a defensive way? Did you consider what you did to create the situation? Do you typically focus on the other person? First, describe your current way of dealing with these accountability situations (**Up to Now**). Then, jot down what you think would be a better way to deal with the situation or circumstance (**From Now On**).

**Up to Now:** When I'm in a situation or a circumstance like this I

_____

_____

_____

_____.

**From Now On:** When I'm in this situation or circumstance I will

_____

_____

_____

_____.

**Stop** Stop being a victim.

Think of a recent situation or circumstance when you went into victim mode. What contributed to your feeling of helplessness? Is it a feeling you routinely experience? Did you do all that you could to avoid the outcome? First, describe your current way of dealing with these accountability situations (**Up to Now**). Then, jot down what you think would be a better way to deal with the situation or circumstance (**From Now On**).

**Up to Now:** When I'm in a situation or a circumstance like this I

_____

_____

_____

_____

_____.

**From Now On:** When I'm in this situation or circumstance I will

_____

_____

_____

_____

_____.

**Stop** **Stop thinking negatively (and masking it by saying you're just keeping it real).**

Think of a recent situation or circumstance when you attempted to mask your negativity by saying that you were just keeping it real. Why did you react this way? Did the other person or group pick up on your negative energy? Is thinking negatively something that you typically do before finding something positive? How is this working for you? First, describe your current way of dealing with these negativity situations (**Up to Now**). Then, jot down what you think would be a better way to deal with the situation or circumstance (**From Now On**).

**Up to Now:** When I'm in a situation or a circumstance like this I

_____

_____

_____

_____

_____.

**From Now On:** When I'm in this situation or circumstance I will

_____

_____

_____

_____

_____.

**Start saying "I got this!" when the going gets tough.**

Think of a recent situation or circumstance when you shied away from assuming responsibility. Why didn't you step up? Was it a situation you experienced before? Were you afraid? Were you worrying about how the other person would react? First, describe your current way of dealing with these accountability situations (**Up to Now**). Then, jot down what you think would be a better way to deal with the situation or circumstance (**From Now On**).

**Up to Now:** When I'm in a situation or a circumstance like this I

_____

_____

_____

_____.

**From Now On:** When I'm in this situation or circumstance I will

_____

_____

_____

_____

_____ .

Start **Start asking for specific, clear feedback for improvement.**

Think of a recent situation or circumstance when you avoided asking for feedback that might have created a different outcome. Why? How do you typically respond to "polish" feedback? What are your thoughts about being a lifelong learner? When are you more receptive to feedback? First, describe your current way of dealing with these feedback situations (**Up to Now**). Then, jot down what you think would be a better way to deal with the situation or circumstance (**From Now On**).

**Up to Now:** When I'm in a situation or a circumstance like this I

_____

_____

_____

_____

_____ .

**From Now On:** When I'm in this situation or circumstance I will

_____

_____

_____

_____

_____ .

**Start listening without judging.**

Think of a recent situation or circumstance when you judged during a conversation rather than listening to what the other person was saying. Why were you judgmental? Are you usually this way? What was it about the other person that contributed to your judgmental behavior? Do you ever consider that you may be wrong? First, describe your current way of dealing with these accountability situations (**Up to Now**). Then, jot down what you think would be a better way to deal with the situation or circumstance (**From Now On**).

**Up to Now:** When I'm in a situation or a circumstance like this I

_____

_____

_____

_____

_____ .

**From Now On:** When I'm in this situation or circumstance I will

_____

_____

_____

_____

_____ .

**Start focusing on the possibility and not the problem.**

Think of a recent situation or circumstance when you focused totally on the obstacle rather than the opportunity. Is this a trend for you? Do you find it easier to focus on what can go wrong rather than what can go right? Do you consider yourself a problem-solver? Do you find that what you focus on grows? First, describe your current way of dealing with life's challenges (**Up to Now**). Then, jot down what you think would be a better way to deal with these situations or circumstances (**From Now On**).

**Up to Now:** When I'm in a situation or a circumstance like this I

_____

_____

_____

_____

_____.

**From Now On:** When I'm in this situation or circumstance I will

_____

_____

_____

_____

_____.

**Start following through with what you said you were going to do.**

Think of a recent situation or circumstance when you disappointed someone because you didn't follow through with what you said you were going to do. What went wrong? Did you overcommit? Is this a trend? How did you rectify the situation? If there was another person involved did he or she accept your apology? Can people trust you? Do people believe in you? First, describe your current way of dealing with these accountability situations (**Up to Now**). Then, jot down what you think would be a better way to deal with the situation or circumstance (**From Now On**).

**Up to Now:** When I'm in a situation or a circumstance like this I

_____

_____

_____

_____ .

**From Now On:** When I'm in this situation or circumstance I will

_____

_____

_____

_____ .

## What's Next?

Now you know how to own your choices. In Winning Way 2, you'll examine the important step of focusing on positive outcomes and expecting success.

## STOP and START Personal Action Plan

STOP using these typical excuses for not owning your choices:

- Well, I didn't mean to do it.
- If someone was offended because of what I said, then I am sorry.
- If she had only done her part things would have worked out.
- If he wasn't so serious he would be able to see that I was only playing.

START using these timely exclamations for owning your choices:

- Beginning today I will own my stuff.
- I will take full responsibility for my intent and for my impact.
- I will examine my past and make the necessary changes. I'm in charge of me.
- It was my fault and I'm going to fix it!

## START, STOP, CONTINUE DOING Habits

Now that you've given some thought to owning your choices as a way to rid your life of excuse making, add other **START Doing, STOP Doing,** and **CONTINUE Doing** habits that will help you attain this goal.

### I will START Doing:

✓ _____
_____

✓ _____
_____

✓ _____
_____

### I will STOP Doing:

✓ _____
_____

✓ _____
_____

✓ _____
_____

| Continue |

### I will CONTINUE Doing:

✓ _____

_____

✓ _____

_____

✓ _____

_____

## Twitter/Facebook Affirmations

Post or tweet your one key takeaway thought, quote, phrase, or lesson learned in this chapter. Enlist your social network community of friends and colleagues to support your efforts to make positive changes in your life.

Make a note of your Twitter or Facebook post here:

_____

_____

_____

_____

_____

# Winning Way 2

## Focus on Positive Outcomes and Expect Success

*Imagination is more important than knowledge.*
—Albert Einstein, physicist and
Nobel Prize winner in physics[1]

Organizations across the world are clamoring for ambitious and creative people who focus on opportunities and not obstacles—people who see the possibilities and not just the problems. In short, people who would absolutely agree with Albert Einstein's approach to work and life.

Unfortunately, these visionary, problem-solving people are harder to find than a contact lens in two feet of snow. Collectively, most of us have lost our ability to see beyond what we believe is wrong, is broken, or won't work or, worse, what we believe is possible. Pessimism and negativity appear to have the upper hand. But so what? You and I are on a personal crusade to change all that and develop a healthier mind-set. So let's get going by dissecting the problem.

## Getting Honest

As I noted in the beginning of this book, it's really hard for us to be honest with ourselves or even others. Even when we know full well we're to blame for a problem—whether it's a minor one or a complete train wreck—we just can't be honest enough to look in the mirror and place the blame where it really belongs.

Admittedly, this approach is effective in some ways. It does absolve you of any blame or responsibility for the problem, and thus you avoid embarrassment or maybe your career stays on track as a result. The downside, however, because you spend all your creative energy and time trying to find ways to blame others, is that you miss the opportunity to offer an effective solution or suggestion to fix the problem or situation. You, and perhaps your organization, just keep rolling along making the same bad decisions. In practical terms, this means that you only focus on:

- What others think about you rather than what you think about yourself—forget having self-esteem.

- Your vulnerabilities and not on your strengths— forget getting picked for the A-team.

- Not standing out and allowing others to shine— forget that promotion or the possibility of developing a valuable friendship or relationship.

- Anger and resentment—forget much of a social life. Who wants to hear all the pessimism, blame, and self-pity you bring to conversations?

Does that sound like a good choice to you? Of course not, and it's not a choice you would consciously make. The fact is, for most of us, our negative attitudes grow over time—one unchallenged, but remembered, insult, rebuff, or put-down at a time, or one missed leadership or take-charge opportunity at a time. It's the seemingly small, insignificant cuts that add up over time to a big problem. By the time we realize that our blaming and excuse habit is allowing others to define who and what we are, it's too late and only those who are truly willing to put the time, sweat, and energy into clawing their way out of the deep excuse hole will ever get out. That's what this book is all about. It's an acknowledgment of your fear and pain, and it's a hand down the long shaft of despair ready to pull you out into a better future.

That's why I offered Albert Einstein's quote at the beginning of this chapter. He nails the idea with powerful simplicity. You must start imagining a different future and more positive outcomes and success no matter what you "know" to be true from past experiences. Imagining a different outcome trumps past experience every time.

## Still, It's Not That Simple

Even with years of experience helping people find new and more productive paths, I still wonder why, in a group of people with similar experiences, grooming, schooling, coaching, or mentoring, some people sink while others soar.

Clearly, an individual's innate ability to maintain a positive attitude no matter what life throws at him or her is a significant piece to this attitude puzzle. I see this dynamic play out all around the world in the seminars and workshops, whether I am speaking to an audience in Beijing, Istanbul, Shanghai, Holland, Singapore, Kuala Lumpur, the Bahamas, Bangalore, or Oslo, or among local clients, friends, or even family members. Once you are stuck in blame mode, it's incredibly hard to switch gears. It's like trying to open a jar with wet hands; traction is nearly impossible to find. From the outside, you can advise, mentor, or coach someone until you are blue in the face about the upside of focusing on what you *do* have rather than what you *don't* have, but until the metaphoric "light" turns on for someone who's caught in the cycle of excuse making, it's nearly impossible for them to break through to the light.

## The Roots of Change

First of all, change begins when we see ourselves as outcome magnets. That's how my mentor Mike Jones—someone who I know focuses on positive outcomes and expects success—frames it. I explained to him my grand "magnet" conclusion after years of believing that focus alone was enough to ensure success and wins in school, in collegiate football, and in business. "'If I keep one eye on the ball and one eye on the goal, I'll surely succeed,' seemed a logical course of action," I told Mike. "Boy was I mistaken. Without the expectation of success—thank you, Norman Vincent Peale and Dr. Wayne Dyer—focus would only take me so far. Focus is mainly about moving forward, not giving up, persistence. I had plenty of that. Expectation provides a direct connection to the world of possibility and it's all about the mystical or perhaps even spiritual idea that the universe is actually rooting for your success if you simply ask for it."

Here's what personal empowerment speaker Rod Hairston has to say in his 2006 book, *Are You Up for The Challenge?* about the idea that whatever you send out is exactly what you will back:

> Instead of wanting not to be poor, you need to hold the thought that you want abundance.... The intensity of emotion behind your thought adds to the strength of the attraction energy. So, the more vividly you picture what you want and the more you ratchet up your enthusiasm about achieving your desired result, the more likely you are to produce it. The intensity of negative emotion works the same way.[2]

Esther and Jerry Hicks, in their book *Ask and It Is Given: Learning to Manifest Your Desires*, offer a similar perspective on expectations:

By the powerful *Law of Attraction*, you draw to you the essence of whatever you are predominantly thinking about. So if you are predominantly thinking about the things that you desire, your life experience reflects those things. And, in the same way, if you are predominantly thinking about what you do not want, your life experience reflects those things.

When you understand the *Law of Attraction*, you are never surprised by what occurs in your experience, for you understand that you have invited every bit of it in—through your own thought process. Nothing can occur in your life experience without your invitation of it through your thought.[3]

Finally, my good friend Trish Uhl, founder and CEO of Owl's Ledge LLC, is what I'd call a living example of the notion that what you think becomes your reality. Here's a compelling, moving story she told me recently that really brings this point home.

Trish's story begins with her waking up in what she thought was a horror movie set. Her skin was swollen and on fire, and not only were her feet in straps, but she also discovered that her body had wire leads connected to a machine. "*It was like waking up in an alien body,*" she told me as a teaser to open up the story of her battle with cancer and the two weeks she had lost in an intensive care unit as doctors and nurses struggled to save her life. The only good news in her diagnosis—an extremely aggressive form of non-Hodgkin's lymphoma—was that it responded well to chemotherapy, even though she said the treatments made her feel like she'd been run over by an 18-wheel transfer truck.

"*Before my hospitalization and cancer diagnosis, my definition of 'success' included doing good work (in my work and community and running a reputable, rewarding consulting business,*" Trish said. "*Waking up in the ICU that day in April, I redefined 'success' to mean basic survival.*" Later, success meant relearning basic human functioning, including elimination (how to go to the bathroom) and how to walk again. "*I wanted my life back,*" Trish told me, and she pushed hard to get it. However, at some point that determination got in the way of her recovery so Trish told me she had to redefine success as "surrendering," to acknowledge how sick she was, so that her focus could be solely on recovery.

"*It was only then that I truly began to heal and started on my journey back to health,*" she said, before adding, "*And I made it back!*" Now, with this experience behind her, Trish sums up her success wisdom this way: "*It took my battle with a catastrophic illness for me to learn that having the appropriate focus and expectation* [of a positive outcome] *will change your life. I know it saved mine.*"

## Exercise

Do you think you can avoid "distraction thinking," and begin to focus positively on the outcome and expect success? If you're ready to move on, then here are a few basic steps that will start you down that path.

**1. Think deeply about your goals.** Get a thorough, clear picture in your head and in your heart of the goal you want to achieve. You should be able to touch it, taste it, smell it, and hear it speak to you. Can you clearly articulate your goal to others? You might surround yourself with pictures and reminders about how you will achieve your goal. I have a vision board hanging on my office wall that I consistently look at throughout the course of the day. I use a standard-size flipchart sheet of paper, positioned to hang on the wall in landscape fashion. Then I use markers along with cutouts from old magazines and tape to start visioning. (The ratio of pictures to my words is about 50/50.) "Jim's Vision Board" is written at the top, and the pictures and words that I place and write on it are a constant source of encouragement and inspiration. I include posts such as the places where I want to speak (Bangkok, India, Kuala Lumpur, Hong Kong, and Europe) in the next few years. I already have commitments to speak in India and Kuala Lumpur in 2012. I also have a note on my board about starting work toward my PhD in 2012.

**2. Remind yourself *why* you want the goal.** *Why?* is one of those great questions we often fail to ask even when it turns out to be the most important question of all. You need to have a clear understanding of why you want to achieve your goal because the *why* drives the actions you take. For example, if you wanted to move, then asking why you want to move out of your home would be an important question. The reason might be to shorten your commute, to find a better school for your children, or to reduce expenses. Stating that you'd like to move without a reason other than you "feel like it," might not pass the motivation, logic, or sanity test.

If you need a little help getting to the *why* of your goal, use the Why Detector Tool Exercise that follows or go to *www.noexcuseguide.com*.

### —Why Detector Tool Exercise—

What's your goal? Write your goal down as clearly and succinctly as possible.

_____

_____

_____

Why is attaining this goal important to you?
List three really good reasons.

1. _____

   _____

2. _____

   _____

3. _____

   _____

Once you obtain or reach your goal, how will
it make you feel?

_____

_____

_____

3. **Visualize yourself obtaining your goal.** Visualization is a much-used technique for one reason: It works. See yourself accepting the diploma. See yourself on the plane going to a destination you desire. See yourself making a successful presentation (you can channel Alex, the Rutgers IEMBA student from the preface, if you wish). See yourself walking down the aisle with your soul mate. See yourself walking into your manager's office to inform her that you have accepted position with another organization. Pretend that you made a video recording of your success, and play it over and over in your head.

The following are some of my favorite techniques to burn your visualized success into your brain and being, using your eyes, mouth, feet, head, and hands:

*Eyes*: I close my eyes and imagine that I see my goal come to fruition. While imagining this scene, I create the time of day, the weather, the season, those with me, and how I feel. I even visualize what I'm wearing and the cologne I have on.

*Mouth*: Share your vision with others. I find that telling others helps me to get clear and focused. It makes me intentional. I imagine the reaction of others and listen to their feedback.

*Feet*: If you can go the place where you want to imagine your success will happen, take the trip. It's a standard part of any presenter's routine to visit the venue of a presentation before the engagement begins. It really does work.

*Head*: While I'm imagining my goal, I think *big*. I'm not just going to fly to India; I'm going to fly first class. I'm not just going to write a book on personal responsibility and accountability; I'm going to write a *New York Times* best-seller.

*Hands*: When I travel, I bring along conversation-starting materials to get more people on my "Dream Team." If someone asks me about the item I'm carrying—a book, a magazine, or even an item of clothing—I use the conversation to engage others in the vision I have.

**4. Change your mental channel to root out pessimistic or negative thoughts.** You change the channel if the show or video you're watching turns out to be terrible, so why not switch the channel in your mind? The key point here is to be in charge of what you choose to focus on. Choose thoughts that will help, not hurt you. Again, I focus on:

- Seeing my workshop participants embracing my message and getting out of their comfort zone.
- Traveling to incredible places to speak and teach.

- Seeing the prospective client nod his head yes, indicating that we have a deal.
- Seeing how I grow spiritually and emotionally with my family.
- Developing ways to reinvent myself and my company and ways to continue to bring value to my clients, customers, and friends.

## 5 Ways to Get Your Focus Back on Track

Even with all the work you do visualizing your success and eliminating excuses from your life, you're bound to get off track. If this happens to you, use the Five R tools to set things right:

1. **Refocus**—by finding a quiet place away from distractions and thinking about your goal and really examine your *why* reasons.

2. **Revisit**—your vision board. Study it and perhaps add to it.

3. **Read**—something powerful and uplifting. Develop a reading list of books, Websites, blogs, and so forth to go to just in case negativity creeps in.

4. **Resist**—the temptation to give voice to any negativity in your mind.

5. **Review**—what you've accomplished thus far on your journey to your goal.

## A Specific Plan

It's all well and good to say you're going to make changes, but you will still need a specific plan to make something happen. Here are some of my favorite techniques to get it done and make a plan.

1. Break down the attainment of your goal into a set of specific steps that must be accomplished to reach your goal.

2. Contact your accountability partners and enlist their support. Perhaps they can help you with your step-by-step list and make valuable suggestions.

3. Establish creative rewards you can give yourself when you reach certain points in your journey toward your goal.

4. Use your social networks (Facebook, Twitter, Team JIMPACT on LinkedIn, or other networks you participate in) to solicit help and advice.

5. Create a business plan for your future success.

6. Contact former coaches or mentors for their guidance.

7. Relax and stop stressing while you regroup and visualize that all is in order and that you're ontrack and moving forward.

## STOP and START Personal Action Plan

STOP using these typical excuses to not focus on positive outcomes and expect success:

- I'm easily distracted.
- It seems like everyone is against me.
- I don't believe in all that "pie-in-the-sky" stuff.
- I can only do one thing at a time. Besides, I don't need help from anyone else. I've always been able to take of things myself.

START using these timely exclamations to focus on positive outcomes and expect success:

- Beginning today I will FOPO (focus on positive outcomes) and ES (expect success)!
- I am not my past!
- I'm not going to see the glass half-empty or half-full. I'm going to see the *pitcher* (or picture) filled to capacity!
- I'm shifting my energy and my mind-set to practice being positive. I'm turning in my fault-finding membership card!

### START, STOP, CONTINUE DOING Habits

Now that you've given some thought to focusing on positive outcomes and expecting success as a way to rid your life of excuse making, add other **START Doing**, **STOP Doing**, and **CONTINUE Doing** habits that will help you attain this goal.

**I will START Doing:**

✓ _____

✓ _____

✓ _____

**I will STOP Doing:**

✓ _____

✓ _____

✓ _____

**I will CONTINUE Doing:**

✓ _____

✓ _____

✓ _____

## Twitter/Facebook Affirmations

Post or tweet your one key takeaway thought, quote, phrase, or lesson learned in this chapter. Enlist your social network community of friends and colleagues to support your efforts to make positive changes in your life.

Make a note of your Twitter or Facebook post here:

_____

_____

_____

_____

_____

# Winning Way 3

## Embrace the Uncertainty

*There is nothing assured to mortals.*
—Horace (65–8 BC), Roman poet[1]

We all know there are no guarantees in life; it's a real "no-brainer" fact of life. Still, for some reason, we just don't want to believe it. Death, taxes, and delayed flights—yes, maybe, we tell ourselves, but for some reason we can't reconcile that there's no one-time special suspension of the rules just for "me."

Sorry. The fix is in. No guarantees. Ever!

However, if it's a 100-percent, money-back, no-questions-asked guarantee you're looking for, then here are a few you can count on and take to the bank any day of the week:

1. You'll keep *getting what you're getting* as long as you keep *doing what you're doing.*

2. Change is inevitable, but growth is optional.

3. You're absolutely going to hear someone complain about *something* today.

I'm sure it would be easy for you to add to this list, but these will do for starters. Frankly, the list of unrealistic, unsupported-by-life's-experience expectations is endless. Just review the list that follows. Do any of these unsupported-by-evidence expectations sound familiar?

- Arriving at work every day on time and performing your job will guarantee your job security.

- Careful and strategic planning and preparation will guarantee that you get a lucrative contract.

- Starting your own business will guarantee a steady stream of paying clients.

- Earning a college degree will guarantee the job you want upon graduation.

- Getting married to the love of your life will guarantee you marital bliss.

Let it go! Life *is* uncertainty! Embrace it and relax and get comfortable with what you really already know. If any of these "happy ending" expectations has any chance of happening, you have to stop making excuses and start doing something to make your expectations a reality.

## How to Embrace Your Fear

Beth Rutter is a good friend of mine. I admire my Canadian buddy for many things, including her career as a regional office manager for a Southern California auto body shop chain. I also admire her for her courage to raise two sons as a single divorced mom, and the "head into the wind, no excuse" way she approaches life and all its uncertainty and fear. Here's what Beth had to say on the subject when I asked her one day about living in fear:

*One of the greatest gifts I ever received was the awareness that what happens in my life is wholly within my control and that the consequences of living in fear were very predictable. That's not to say I don't experience fear—I do—sometimes on a daily basis. In fact, that sinking feeling in the pit of my stomach has become my barometer for where I need to go next whether in my personal or professional life. I have received so many unexpected gifts that would never have been available to me had I given in to my fears. Plus, the cool thing about [facing your fear] is that the more I do it, the better I get at it! If my children only learn this one thing from me then I will consider my time here well spent. I know that if I just give my all at every turn I will always be able to look back and say, "Yup—at least I had the guts to go for it at every opportunity."*

Clearly, Beth has a well-developed "go for it" mind-set that compels her to fly right into the face of uncertainty and assures her that she's doing absolutely the right thing. Unfortunately, most of us have trouble overriding our programmed "fight or flight" mind-set, designed to shield us from any physical or emotional consequences that may result from our decisions.

According to Dr. Neil F. Neimark's December 2011 article, "The Fight or Flight Response," the flight or fright response was originally discovered by Harvard physiologist Walter Cannon, who found that this response was hardwired into our brains and is "a genetic wisdom designed to protect us from bodily harm." He notes that "this response actually corresponds to an area of our brain called the hypothalamus, which—when stimulated—initiates a sequence of nerve cell firing and chemical release that prepares our body for running or fighting."[2]

"This fundamental physiologic response," according to Dr. Neimark, "forms the foundation of modern day stress medicine. The 'fight or flight response' is our body's primitive, automatic, inborn response that prepares the body to 'fight' or 'flee' from perceived attack, harm, or threat to our survival."[3] He continues:

When our fight or flight system is activated, we tend to perceive everything in our environment as a possible threat to our survival. By its very nature, the fight or flight system bypasses our rational mind—where our more well thought out beliefs exist—and moves us into "attack" mode. This state of alert causes us to perceive almost everything in our world as a possible threat to our survival. As such, we tend to see everyone and everything as a possible enemy...we are on the lookout for every possible danger. We may overreact to the slightest comment. Our fear is exaggerated. Our thinking is distorted. We see everything through the filter of possible danger...fear becomes the lens through which we see the world.[4]

## The New Normal World

I see this innate fear manifested in today's chaotic, uncertain workplace. Even with an improving economy, due to the downsizing, right-sizing, and layoffs that have defined many organizations over the last few years, most of us harbor some fear in our minds that we might just be the next one shown the door. This fear drives many of the behaviors discussed throughout this book, such as blaming others, not taking responsibility, the need to control everything, the need to be right no matter what (chasing perfection), distracted listening, and the lack of job or life satisfaction and passion for living.

Unfortunately, the crazy, confusing, and frightening world we live in today is here to stay. It's the "new normal," and I'm afraid we're all required to be flexible and find a way to make it work—or, as a plain-spoken coach, mentor, or friend might say, "You're going to have to suck it up and keep going!"

Living in the new normal conditions means we must learn to lean into our discomfort and forget the old comfort zones of the past. Your parents may have worked at the same job for 30 or even 40 years, but that world is gone for good. If you think you'll be able to keep your same job even for the next five years or that you'll be doing the same job five years from now in the same department, under the same boss, who expects the same level of performance, I suggest you think again. You know this, but I'll say it anyway: It just isn't gonna happen.

*—Quick Uncertainty Quiz—*

The first step to get a handle on uncertainty is to name the things that worry you. Take a minute and jot down the things that are creating uncertainty for you (professionally or personally) right now. You can list them here in the book or electronically on your computer, tablet, or other device. You can also print out copies of this and other exercises and assessments by visiting *www.noexcuseguide.com*.

Once you've identified your fears and uncertainty, determine how many of them you have direct control over. Do you think changing your mind-set might play a significant role in creating results different from those you normally expect? Write your thoughts down in the column provided next to the fear/uncertainty column. You'll find more tips on how to manage your doubt and fear as you move through this book to help you become a "go for it" player in the game of life.

| I am uncertain and fearful because ____. | Despite the fear and uncertainty, I can take positive action by _____. |
|---|---|
| 1. | |
| 2. | |
| 3. | |
| 4. | |
| 5. | |
| 6. | |

## Managing Fear and Doubt

The fact that you recognize that you allow your fear and uncertainty to win way too often is a good sign that you're on your way to leading a fearless life. As you know by now, most excuse making is just a convenient way to keep your terror at bay. You are already beginning to see that waiting for someone else to fix your problems or lead you to success isn't working. So, how do you move forward and start making positive changes? It's not as hard as you think. In fact, answers to this question are found almost anywhere you look. You just have to be ready to accept the answers and stay open to the possibilities.

Johnny B. Truant is a small business consultant who takes a unique approach toward what is needed for business success. His brand of "punk rock business consultant" pretty well provides all the definition that is needed to get an idea of his approach. Truant also is a guest blogger for several entrepreneurial sites, and his communities of readers look forward to his pithy, inspirational, and instructive advice. Here's an abbreviated version of an October 24, 2011, blog post directed toward entrepreneurs. It's called "6 Ways to Master Entrepreneurial Uncertainty," and it's certainly appropriate to any discussion about facing uncertainty and fear.

1. Embrace uncertainty.

   *Certainty* is a cage. Sure, we all like that warm feeling that comes from knowing where we are and what's coming next, but that's not the way life is meant to be lived 24/7....

2. Uncouple fear from uncertainty.

   The knee-jerk reaction to uncertainty is fear.... [E]ven though uncertainty often brings fear, uncertainty is not the same as fear.

3. Acknowledge fear, and hear what it is trying to tell you.

> Look your fear square in the eye.... It's saying, "This might happen, so plan accordingly." But— and this is key—make sure you don't believe fear knows more than it does about the future....

4. Do something.

> Action is the antidote to fear. If you're uncertain and afraid, the worst thing you can do is to simply wait to see what happens. Do something. Do *anything*....

5. Be courageous.

> Fear is normal. Proceeding in the face of that fear is the courage you need in order to grow and to become more.

6. Live and learn from fear.

> ...[T]he key to being amazing is doing the things that frighten you.

## My Own Run-In With Fear

For me, my fear factor was in low gear when I left a secure, full-time job to start JIMPACT Enterprises. I had been thinking about starting my own company for some time and colleagues at all the companies on my resume—Prudential, Vanguard, CoreStates Bank, Simmons Associates, and The Bob Pike Group—were all supportive of the idea.

So when I left my own comfort zone in the corporate world to expand my skills as a speaker and trainer, I just knew that eventually I'd be successful at honing my own brand of high-energy, passionate, and empowering training.

My uncertainty period kicked in about midway through my first year, when nearly all the work I'd been promised disappeared like sale items on Black Friday. Instead of reacting in a positive way, I let my uncertainty turn my days into a "tension convention." I started focusing more on paying bills than I did on securing opportunities. I spent more time talking to creditors than I did clients. I even thought about giving up on my business.

Then one day, it all changed. It wasn't that clients suddenly starting pouring in or that I found a secret stash of cash to keep the business going. No, my business changed when *I changed.* I put away my "woe is me" violin, and stopped playing the victim and blame game. I stopped relying on others to solve my problems. I started to look at my situation as a challenge—and I love challenges as much as I love seafood, jerk chicken, and the beach. I started operating out of a place of abundance—that is, I started acting, every day, like I had already arrived and that everything was going great. I decided to become Mr. Energy! My morning mantra was "I've got some JIMPACTing to do today!"

When I channeled my uncertainty toward building passion, enthusiasm, and creativity, everything changed. The energy in my voice changed. The enthusiasm in my voicemail greeting changed. I welcomed calls from creditors, and suddenly the calls were friendlier. My mojo returned and I succeeded.

## Handling Uncertainty Is Good for Creativity

According to a study cited by Jonathan Fields in his 2011 book, *Uncertainty: Turning Fear and Doubt into Fuel for Brilliance*, not knowing for sure what awaits you can be a powerful tool to increase creativity. According to the 2008 *Journal of Creative Behavior* study he cited, ambiguity is "significantly and positively" related to creativity.[6] Who knew?

# My Super Six Tenets for Eliminating Fear

So, do I have still fight fear? Of course; no one gets a free pass on this one. But what I have that helps me is a structured way to turn my own fear of uncertainty toward a positive result. I have developed these six tenets to help me keep fear at bay. You can adopt or adapt these, or develop your own; these points work for me. I share them in my personal power sessions, and I even highlight them when I conduct presentation skills workshops and train-the-trainer sessions.

Here are my Super Six Tenets for shifting my mind-set when I need to embrace uncertainty, doubt, and fear:

1. **Meditate.** I meditate for 30 minutes every morning right after my daily devotion. For me, it's just part of getting centered and balanced for the day, and it includes a spiritual connection in the form of a prayer. You'll have to determine what prayer means for you and how it might help you with positive mind cleansing (for example, deleting any negative thoughts and thinking about how you're going to put a positive spin on everything you do for the day).

2. **Train and feed your mind.** I will not allow my mind to think negatively or have "what if this went wrong?" thoughts. If I'm moving toward a WWW (wallow, whine, or worry) state, I quickly block out that pathway to negativity. This does not make me completely immune to negativity, but there is a negativity tipping point, and I do everything I can do to stay on the positive side.

3. **Connect with your spiritual side.** Spiritual, for me, is reading from a Bible or checking out a Bible quote app on my Android. Clearly, there are many ways to be spiritual and connect to this side of your humanity. No matter what connection you choose, I believe making this effort helps center and calm you for the success you expect to happen.

4. **Create a positive "store room."** For me, having a physical place that signifies and holds empowering energy is a key resource. That's why I have a room in my home devoted to storing and displaying all things positive, whether the inspiration comes from books, posters, music, or movies. I go there to reenergize. If you don't have an extra room, even a corner of a room or dedicated bookshelf will work.

5. **Nurture your butterflies.** Celebrate the moments when you get those butterflies before a presentation, or even speaking up at a meeting or attempting something new. Don't panic! Don't run from the feeling. Embrace your nervous jitters. Even after all these years of speaking before thousands of people, my butterflies return. I've learned to love the butterflies, and I use them to help me

make an even better presentation. You can do the same, whether it's facing an uncomfortable situation at work, or having an important or difficult conversation with your spouse or teenage son or daughter.

6. **Examine the story you are telling.** Many of us live in stories and not in facts. The stories we tell ourselves evolve from our perceptions of what happens to us. You are not the sum of your credit score, and your value is not based on someone else's opinion of you. Are you giving others too much power over your personal story? You are the director and screenwriter of your own movie, so make sure you write the script that you want.

## Eliminating Fear Exercise

What will you use as your standard practice (tenets) to eliminate fear and uncertainty from your life? You don't have to use the same tenets I use, but I do believe it is important that you establish regular habits that protect you from negative ways of thinking and the excuse making that results. Jot down your own tenets for eliminating fear in the space provided here or visit *www.noexcuseguide.com* to download this and other exercises used in this book.

| My Tenets for Eliminating Fear and Uncertainty | *Brief description of the practice and how you'll implement the practice into your life.* |
|---|---|
| 1. | |
| 2. | |
| 3. | |
| 4. | |
| 5. | |

## Conclusion

Do you think you are ready to face down your fears and make uncertainty your friend? Are you ready to open yourself to a more fulfilling and purposeful life? Then come from behind the curtain of life. Hide your safety net. Let go of what he, she, and they said. Climb to the top of the mountain, take a deep breath, and *jump* into your joy. As the famous Swiss psychiatrist Carl Gustav Jung framed the issue: "I am not what happened to me—I am what I choose to become."[7]

## STOP and START Personal Action Plan

STOP using these typical excuses for not embracing the uncertainty:

- Who's to say everything is going to work out?
- That's just not me.
- No one in my family has ever done that.
- Statistics suggests that the odds are not in my favor.

START using these timely exclamations for embracing the uncertainty:

- Here I go!
- I'll show you!
- I'm sick and tired of being sick and tired!
- I can do this. No, I WILL do this!

### START, STOP, CONTINUE DOING Habits

Now that you've given some thought to embracing your fear and uncertainty as a way to rid your life of excuse making, add other **START Doing**, **STOP Doing**, and **CONTINUE Doing** habits that will help you attain this goal.

**Start**

## I will START Doing:

✓ _____

_____

✓ _____

_____

✓ _____

_____

**Stop**

## I will STOP Doing:

✓ _____

_____

✓ _____

_____

✓ _____

_____

**Continue**

## I will CONTINUE Doing:

✓ _____

_____

✓ _____

_____

✓ _____

_____

## Twitter/Facebook Affirmations

Post or tweet your one key takeaway thought, quote, phrase, or lesson learned in this chapter. Enlist your social network community of friends and colleagues to support your efforts to make positive changes in your life.

Make a note of your Twitter or Facebook post here:

_____

_____

_____

_____

_____

# Winning Way 4

## Do More With Your Best

*Our business in life is not to get ahead of others, but to get ahead of ourselves—to break our own records, to outstrip our yesterday by our today.*
—Stewart B. Johnson, Scottish painter[1]

Even before the 2009 "great recession" took up long-term residency in our economy, the no-fault work environment was a well-established and accepted fact of life whereby we now work in a "no one owes you anything" workplace environment.

I don't need to tell you that most companies that managed to survive this latest economic meltdown won't be trying out a more "traditional" organizational model anytime soon. For the foreseeable future you'll be living in a "new normal" business and workplace reality. It's an environment that may seem like a broken record of business catchphrases and euphemisms, such as doing more with less, right-sizing, and rethinking our business model.

Even as the business environment improves and unemployment slowly moves downward, solid individual contributors, tenured leaders, and savvy newcomers to underperforming companies with potential for growth are sometimes forced to make the slow walk to human resources for an exit interview. In short, it's still not a pretty picture out there for millions of workers.

However, just because we "know" something to be true doesn't necessarily mean we change our behavior to match the reality we face. So, instead of facing up to facts, we usually gravitate toward playing the "why can't things be the way they used to?" game, and then complain and whine about what is fair, right, and acceptable. If you recognize the painful sting of truth when it hits you in the face, then perhaps it's time for a change.

To make my point through a sports analogy, imagine this familiar locker room scenario. You are in the middle of a sporting event (football, basketball, soccer, field hockey—you pick). You know the game is going so badly because you notice your home team fans streaming out of the stadium (or building) as you head for the locker room at halftime. Your coach summons you and the rest of the players together in the crowded space between two rows of lockers and in measured, sincere tones delivers more unwelcome news: Not only is your team getting clobbered, but your star player is injured and won't be playing in the second half of the game.

Suddenly, the solemn locker room mood is broken. A cacophony of whines and curses pours forth from you and your team members. The coach allows the self-flagellation to go on for about 30 seconds, and then holds up a hand, frowning slightly to emphasize the "okay, that's enough" message. When the room quiets down and all eyes are trained on the coach, he delivers a rousing pep talk as good as any you've seen on stage or screen.

"Listen up!" the coach begins, emphasizing his resolve by firmly planting a foot on the only unoccupied part of the long bench running between the sets of lockers. "I know it's a bad break, but that's the way it is. We just have to play with the players we have. It does us no good to focus on the player we're missing. As you know, in sports and in life, you're not always going to get the best hand; things are not always going to happen as planned. But you have to look at the situation as an opportunity—yes, an opportunity—for you to dig deep and find resources, resolve, and courage that you never thought you had!"

"Today," the coach says, focusing directly on you, "I need more than your A- game—more than even your A-plus game. When you head back out on that field, I need you to do even better. I need you to play with more intensity, more passion, and more drive than you can imagine. We simply are not going to lose; I don't care what the score is! Elevate your game to a higher level. I know you can do it! Remember: The team that wants to win the most is the team that will walk away with the trophy! So, how bad do you want it?"

Everyone stands up and cheers, promising to meet the coach's challenge. The coach throws the ball your way. You catch it confidently and then raise the ball high with your right arm, the obvious answer made with your gesture.

"Absolutely, Coach!" you nearly shout in answer. "I know we can do it! No, make that we *will* do it! I want it so bad that I can nearly taste it," you tell the coach. Cheers erupt as the rest of the team stands up. Spontaneously, your team-mates run toward the door high-fiving each other as they squeeze through the narrow, impossibly small, escape route.

## How Bad Do You Want It?

How committed are you to changing your current situation? Are you behaving like one of the players in our fictional locker room? Are you taking charge and creating a new playbook and reality for your team? Remember: It's the choices that *you* make that matter the most.

This is a question that I pose to my audiences all over the world. It's a powerful question if you think about it. If you can truly answer the question, "How bad do you want it?" straight from the heart, then you've just begun the complete transformation of the rest of your life. Like your wise, imagined coach pointed out to you, there's little mileage to be gained in today's workplace or life by whining or making excuses. Are you up for the challenge of living in an imperfect world? If you are, then it's time to stand toe-to-toe with even the biggest roadblocks to your success and breeze right past! Here's the simple set of instructions you need to facilitate this fateful meeting with your future and destiny.

### —Taking Charge Exercise—

1. Find the largest and most conveniently located mirror you can find. A clothing store mirror (men or women's) is the best for this exercise. Most of these mirrors allow you to step into a three-sided box so that you can check out how good you look. Of course, a standard bathroom mirror will do fine, but there is an advantage to the "nowhere to hide" feeling communicated by a bank of mirrors all trained on you!

2. Step directly in front of your chosen mirror. Place your feet firmly on the floor, and bend your legs slightly so that you have a good sense of balance and stability. Relax your shoulders, close your eyes, and take a nice long, cleansing breath. Let your breath out slowly; then open your eyes to face the mirror.

3. Make direct eye contact with the person you see in the mirror (or the multiple people around you, if you're lucky enough to have found an

unoccupied clothing store mirror). Stare as intently as possible while you clear your mind of all thoughts.

4. Raise your right hand to a position directly in front of your chest and extend your index finger. Point the finger directly at the image in the mirror and repeat these words: "It's your move!"

5. Repeat the exercise until you really "get" it! If you need assistance or convincing (about where to place the responsibility), you can ask the store clerk (or your spouse, significant other, or friend) after you've shared with him your challenge, but I suspect he will agree that it really is your call.

If you want to practice using the previous empowerment technique, think through this scenario:

You're the last person to interview for a job. The panel of six interviewers are exhausted and they don't want to hear from you, but they must because you're on the agenda. When you walk in they look at you with thinly disguised disdain as you take a seat across from the six critical, unsympathetic inquisitors. What are you going to do? How might you convince them they saved the best for last?

## No Outside Answers

I spend a great majority of my nonspeaking, consulting, and training time helping people break the cycle of blame and excuse making. I often think that it's easier to become a Navy Seal than to get people to take personal responsibility for their future. It's just hard to motivate my audiences and clients to get off the dime and take action. One of my favorite "mental tools" is the idea of a "reset" button.

The reset idea occurred to me one morning when I mounted my exercise bike for a 60-minute ride. I followed my usual habit of sitting squarely on the seat before adjusting the toe cages and pedal straps. Then, I looked down at the illuminated ride option button to select a workout (interval, aerobic, manual, time distance, speed, etc.). As I reached for the aerobic setting, I noticed a button I had previously ignored: the reset button! "That's it," I thought. "Just stop what you're doing and hit the reset button to take a fresh look at your life and circumstances and the decisions we make."

## Hit the Reset Button

I used this revelation when I applied the reset button to see how I marketed my services. Instead of focusing on only large companies, I decided that no opportunity was too small or insignificant to consider. So, when the owner of my wife's hair salon asked me to run an empowerment session for his employees, I said yes. That decision led me to a much larger and more lucrative consulting opportunity as a result of a serendipitous encounter with one of the salon's regular clients.

The reset button also prompted me to investigate teaching at a local university, and this new thinking led me to Temple and Rutgers University National and International Executive MBA programs and the opportunity to teach my course on executive global leadership in Beijing, Shanghai, and Singapore.

## Get Out the Negative Energy

Still, clever new ways of thinking will only take you so far. In order to do more with your best, you must turn these creative forms of expression into consistent action backed by positive energy and expression. You must create a mental picture of a positive future and chase away negativity that fuels nothing but negative results. Getting out the negative energy means that you must see yourself leveraging even long-dormant skills and listen for all the praise and recognition directed toward you. As mentioned earlier, our mind-set drives our behaviors and our results.

## 9 Vital Aspects of Success

I recently asked some of my clients and workshop participants to list what they thought was vital for success in today's workforce. This list highlights the nine most noted characteristics:

1. Self-awareness.
2. Lifestyle balance.
3. Resiliency.
4. Positive attitude.
5. Adaptability.
6. Purposefulness.
7. Critical thinking.
8. Confidence.
9. Versatility.

Though this is a great list, my work with people and organizations over the years leads to me suggest (and highlight/amend) a few other critical factors that will help you create even more value and do more with your best, including the following.

## Self-Management

Organizations are looking for people who don't need a lot of direction and confirmation; they want people who can manage themselves and execute priorities in an effective and efficient way. Trust me: Everything counts. How well you manage yourself during meetings and disagreements, times of change, and distractions is carefully noted, if not measured. Organizations want proactive, assertive, and poised leaders, not insecure and toxic complainers. However, you have to still be fully in charge of staying motivated and energized, even if your boss gives praise and feedback sparingly. It can be a difficult balancing act.

## Presentation Skills

If you think about it, we are always on stage (formally or informally). An effective presenter is able to connect with a listener's head and heart, whether it's an audience of one person or 500. Never waste your "privilege of the platform" opportunities. Upgrade your presentation skills on all levels.

## Volunteerism

Consider volunteer opportunities that take you out of your comfort zone. Not only does this effort create exposure opportunities, but volunteering affords you a chance to showcase your skills and obtain new ones. The line for acquiring "performance-stretch marks" is not usually very long.

## Decision-Making

Although I agree that critical thinking is at least a subset of decision-making, many in today's professional workforce are uniquely empowered to create their own outcomes and to make the right decisions concerning their business partners, vendors, and peers. Leadership appreciates individuals who are able to put out organizational fires, rather than wasting time talking or meeting about the inferno or, worse, trying to find someone to blame.

## Appearance, Presence, and Image

How do you show up for work and life? Are you engaged mentally, physically, and emotionally? When people see you, what do they see? Although the "dress for success" rules have changed, appearance is still important. Even if your organization's official or unofficial policy is business casual, your choice should still be professional. Believe me: It matters! Sorry to break the news, but promotions are not solely based on performance. Your appearance, presence, and image are critical factors for your success. A tattoo, excessive facial hair, multiple ear piercings, a tight skirt, or funky hair color could cloud leadership's perception of your work. Does the energy in the meeting room or even lunchroom increase when you enter? For some people, the energy increases when they exit the door, and trust me when I say that you don't want to be that person.

## Authenticity

I often wondered what the workplace would be like if everyone told the truth—if everyone came clean. I'm not suggesting personal attacks; those are easy to do and are more about not taking responsibility. What I am suggesting is making a difference in your organization by developing a reputation for integrity, candor, and trust. You want to be known as someone who does not sugarcoat the truth to avoid confrontation or retribution by not agreeing with your manager. Develop a reputation as someone your leaders know they can count on to be forthright and genuine, regardless of the consequences.

## Networking

Many people think that active and purposeful net-working is a self-serving activity. In some ways, it is—but so what? Networking has another, more altruistic side, and that's helping other people meet their needs as well. Here are some pointers on effective networking that will ensure that everyone benefits from the relationship:

- Understand the other person's needs.
- Be an effective listener and you'll be an effective networker.
- Provide and bring value to the connection.
- Don't dismiss anyone as irrelevant.
- Follow up and follow through with your promises.
- Provide connections beyond your industry or organization.
- Networking is best in person and face-to-face (but social networking can work just fine, so use it).

## Attitude

Your attitude will take you where you want to go. Your *attitude* will determine your success *altitude*. As Winston Churchill said, "Attitude is a little thing that makes a BIG difference."[2] It's your choice. Besides, who would you rather hang around: someone with a downbeat, negative attitude, or someone who is positive and who looks for positive solutions at work and in her life?

## Follow-Through

Consistent follow-through is about choice, focus, discipline, and integrity. You can distinguish yourself among your peers by simply doing what you say you're going to do. When you take on a task, make sure you know what the expectations are, and create some way to ensure that you complete the assignment (to-do lists, pop-up messages on your computer, and reminders on your cell phone). Frankly, you won't find much sympathy for excuses. If it will help, develop a *feedback contract* with those to whom you make commitments. A feedback contract is simply a pact you make with someone regarding how you're going to give and receive feedback, both positive and constructive.

## Relationship Building

Connect, connect, and connect. Author and poet Maya Angelou summed up the power of relationships when she said, "People may not remember what you said and people may not remember what you did, but, people will remember how you made them feel."[3] Even in a society dominated by social media and electronic communication, the real, honest, and connected relationships you build with others will ultimately determine your success. As Maribeth Kuzmeski notes in her book, *The Connectors: How the World's Most Successful Businesspeople Build Relationships and Win Clients for Life*:

> The ability to connect is a different kind of intelligence, one that is the proverbial icing on the cake for most of the people who have reached to high levels of greatness; it simply requires that you focus on others and have a plan to serve them, pay attention to them, listen to them and care about them. The key determinant at the top of all business strategies, talents and expertise is the ability to connect with people on a meaningful level—one that produces quality associations and profitable business relationships.[4]

## Leadership

The best leaders create an empowering environment of enablement and enthusiasm. They strive to build relationships and create a shared vision that goes beyond the bounds of organizational level, race, gender, education, culture, ethnicity, experience, sexual orientation, physical and/or mental ability, veteran's status, marital or parental status, class, or age. Great leaders challenge minds and encourage creativity. They reward and recognize and seek to ensure both personal and professional development. What kind of leader do you want to be? It's easy to figure out the most successful model to follow.

# Doing More With Your Best

Even professional speakers can do more with their best. A little more than nine years ago I attended a workshop put on by consultant Doug Stevenson, a well-known expert on storytelling. (Learn more at *www.storytheater.com*.) I thought my skills were pretty good, but the workshop sounded interesting, so I attended and learned how much I really didn't know.

For the three days I was there, I was pushed, prodded, and challenged to excel and go beyond my best. The experience left me humbled and uplifted at the same time. I guess Coach John Wooden was right when he commented, "It's what you learn after you know it all that counts."[5] That's what doing more with your best is all about.

## STOP and START Personal Action Plan

STOP using these typical excuses for not doing more with your best:

- It doesn't make a difference what I do. Management has their mind made up anyway.

- I tried to change before, but nothing happened.

- There aren't any jobs out there. Besides, I have to pay my bills.

- I'm tired of changing for somebody else. When are they going to change for me?

START using these timely exclamations for doing more with your best:

- Beginning today I will shift my mind-set to get the results that I want.

- Change is a door that can only be opened from the inside. I will give my-self 30 days to do some rearranging.

- I will reset and acquire some reset part-ners to help keep me on track.

- I see the value in adjusting my perfor-mance to thrive in this "new normal." I'm up for the challenge.

### START, STOP, CONTINUE DOING Habits

Now that you've given some thought to doing more with your best as a way to rid your life of excuse making, add other **START Doing**, **STOP Doing**, and **CONTINUE Doing** habits that will help you attain this goal.

**Start**

## I will START Doing:

✓ _____

_____

✓ _____

_____

✓ _____

_____

**Stop**

## I will STOP Doing:

✓ _____

_____

✓ _____

_____

✓ _____

_____

**Continue**

## I will CONTINUE Doing:

✓ _____

_____

✓ _____

_____

✓ _____

_____

## Twitter/Facebook Affirmations

Post or tweet your one key takeaway thought, quote, phrase, or lesson learned in this chapter. Enlist your social network community of friends and colleagues to support your efforts to make positive changes in your life.

Make a note of your Twitter or Facebook post here:

_____

_____

_____

_____

_____

# Winning Way 5

## Listen With Three Ears

*It's a rare person who wants to hear what
he doesn't want to hear.*
—Dick Cavett, entertainer and comedian[1]

Poor listening habits are responsible for many of our daily woes. Whether it's a damaging disagreement with a co-worker, a miscommunication with a spouse or partner, or an awful customer service experience, the smoking gun is often a simple failure to pay attention—to truly listen to what the other person is saying.

Sure, it's easy to develop techniques to help you remember *what* people say—that's "two-ear" listening—and perhaps if we did that we'd all have fewer disagreements with our colleagues, family, and friends. But better two-ear listening will only take you so far. If you really want to take listening at a more life-changing level and impact your excuse-making habit, then developing your heart-based "third-ear" listening skills is absolutely essential.

Of course, third-ear listening requires more energy, so before you decide if this *super*-listening might be too hard—and start searching for a way out—perhaps I should explain a bit more about third-ear listening.

## What Is Third-Ear Listening?

First, if you listen with your "third ear," then you don't filter what you hear with supposition, stereotypes, judgment, what someone else said, and bitterness. You don't let past experiences with someone limit your ability to truly empathize with someone else's "life load." Third-ear listening also means engaging and connecting with another human being on an emotional, even spiritual level. My good friend, colleague, and personal coach since 2003, Annie Hart is founder and CEO of Breakthrough Coaching, Training and Storytelling, an NLP trainer and NVC (nonviolent communication) practitioner, and the former CEO of the consulting firm Heartworks, agrees with the potential power of third-ear listening. She put it this way during our interview:

> If you really want to connect, understand, and influence other people you need the power of listening from the heart. What I mean by the heart is not the idea of something weak or emotional. The heart energy is actually the source of strength and balance in the body. The heart is a brain, far more powerful than the head brain. If you really want to connect, you are going to need the empathetic power of the heart.

## Teaching About the Third Ear

As a business and personal coach and speaker, I see the power of making this primal listening connection through my interactions with diverse groups of people and individual clients around the world. For example, each year when I teach my Rutgers International Executive MBA (IEMBA) global leadership course in China, I face a diverse group of engineers, project leaders, programmers, and consultants who are accustomed to using their analytic left brain at work more than their interpersonal right brain. Frankly, I can see in their eyes at the outset of my classes that they'd rather be giving a lion a "mani-pedi" than be in my classroom. These students know that for two weeks, no economics, statistics, business analysis, spreadsheets, marketing strategies, research projects, or pie charts will be discussed. Instead, they know they'll be required to use their "heart" connection to lead, develop, manage, and build relationships with the teams and individual performers.

Slowly over those two weeks, I watch the left-brained future captains of industry "get it," and I observe a profound shift in their attitude as they fully understand the power of managing and listening from the heart. By the last day of the class, when the students are asked to participate in the Relic exercise, everyone is sold on the idea of third-ear listening and managing with the concept in mind.

The Relic exercise, by the way, requires participants to bring one extremely significant item to class, such as an artifact, a piece of jewelry, a book, or a photograph, and to discuss its significance in front of all the other students. Each student is asked to first speak from the heart about the significant item. Before the next person shares his Relic, he must first demonstrate that he was listening with his engaged and empathetic third ear by first connecting with one of the themes (family, travel, education, etc.) of the previous presenter's presentation. Invariably, many students say this exercise is the most powerful and meaningful one of my course.

Annie told me recently:

*Everyone has a deep desire to be heard and understood. Listening through the heart strengthens teamwork, reduces stress and conflict, and has many other benefits. It is especially unifying for people who work together. Our typical style of communication is to interrupt, ask questions, or offer advice. Deep listening has you be silent, attentive, and calm. To do this you need to remain balanced and neutral. You don't need to offer your opinion or advice. In fact, the less you say the better; when you put all of your attention on someone, something very profound changes.*

*Deep listening is about paying attention. It's a process of truly hearing and understanding another's point of view. Though it sounds like a simple skill, it's not. Most of the time when we are listening, we are really hearing the thoughts in our own head. The secret to deep listening is that you listen through another's map, not your own. In this way, you truly put the other person first. This is the most profound way to truly connect with anyone in any situation. It is the most important skill I know.*

Clearly, Annie is an expert third-ear listener who admits that the skill is not immediately accessible. In fact, even now she says she is constantly refining and practicing her skills. Now that you understand what third-ear listening means, here's a brief skill-builder exercise that will enable you to start tuning in your enhanced listening skills.

*—Listening With the Third Ear Exercise—*

This exercise has two phases: narrative and application.

## Phase One: Narrative

Complete the following sentences:

I typically stop listening when someone

_____

_____

_____

_____ .

I'm a better listener when someone

_____

_____

_____

_____ .

People at work would say my listening skills are _____ (good/okay/terrible). Please explain:

_____

_____

_____

_____ .

People at home would say my listening skills are _____ (good/okay/terrible). Please explain:

_____

_____

_____

_____ .

I interrupt people during conversations when I

_____

_____

_____

_____ .

When someone interrupts me I feel _____ . Explain why you feel this way:

_____

_____

_____

_____ .

People can tell I've stopped listening because I

_____

_____

_____

_____ .

When it comes to listening with my third ear, I know I have to

_____

_____

_____

_____ .

Listening with my third ear will help me

_____

_____

_____

_____ .

## Phase Two: Application

1. My "head and heart" coach Annie Hart says that "*to connect with someone else, you need to understand their thoughts, feelings, and [their] map of the world. You simply cannot understand someone from your point of view.*" The best listeners understand the power of empathy—how to *understand another person.*

   **Exercise instructions:** Stop reading at this point. Place a call to someone you think would say you're not a great listener. Based on the information you just read, practice listening with your third ear on this call. No excuses; no ifs, ands, or buts. Just listen intently and then, after the call, write down what that experience was like for you and what you think it was like for the person you called.

2.  Stephen Covey, author of the best-selling book *The 7 Habits of Highly Successful People*, says, "Most people do not listen with the intent to understand; they listen with the intent to reply."[2]

    **Exercise instructions:** Think of someone (your spouse, partner, boss, friend, etc.) you need to have a one-on-one meeting with. Think about a topic you often get into with him or her that is always left unresolved or that creates tension or frustration. Have a meeting with that person. Bring up the topic and practice listening with your third ear during the conversation. Remember what Covey said, and don't listen with the intent to reply. After the conversation, write down what that experience was like for you and what you think it was like for the other person.

3.  Dr. Marie Amey-Taylor, a former assistant vice president in the human resources department, learning and development division of Temple University and now a member of the JIMPACT team, says that listening with the third ear means resisting the temptation to anticipate what someone is going to say. During our interview she said this distracted listening can happen due to either perceived differences or similarities. In both instances, Dr. Amey-Taylor said, "*You tend to* [run ahead and] *finish their sentences and both of these* [tendencies] *are bad habits that cause you to miss information.*"

**Exercise instructions:** Reach out to someone who reports to you or someone whose life you would say that you play a leadership role (a child, a direct report, a team member, etc.). You can call or meet one-on-one. Bring up a subject that you believe, in spite of her superior knowledge and experience, you still know more about. Practice listening with your third ear. Remember what Dr. Amey-Taylor said: Don't anticipate what the other person is going to say or finish her sentences. After the conversation write down what that experience was like for you and what you think it was like for her.

When you're finished with the conversations, resume reading.

## Why We Don't Listen

Whether you blame the educational system, human nature that dismisses or devalues the unfamiliar, or our distracted, too-connected, too-much-information society, the result is the same: No one seems to be listening. (See the end of this chapter for a convenient list of excuses to use.)

According to the December 2011 article "Listening Skills: A Powerful Key to Successful Negotiating," statistics indicate that the normal, untrained listener is likely to understand and retain only about 50 percent of a conversation. This relatively poor percentage drops to an even less-impressive 25-percent retention rate 48 hours later.[3] This means that recall of particular conversations will usually be inaccurate and incomplete.

What blurs your listening vision? When I consider my listening track record, I can remember countless times when I shut down, got defensive, or disengaged. The common denominator for me was usually anger, agitation, impatience, resentment, bias, or the desire to be right (discussed further in Winning Way 8). I know my body attended those conversations, but my mind and empathetic, supportive third ear went for a walk.

I remember one particular sales call from a couple of years ago that I didn't get because I clearly was not listening to the client. Throughout the meeting I was given plenty of clues as to how I should steer the conversation if I wanted the work, yet I kept right on talking, selling my services and preferred approach, and not listening. When I didn't get the job, I resisted the temptation to find a convenient excuse and instead asked the potential client. That call confirmed what I deep down already knew: I wasn't listening and it cost me plenty.

Can you recall similar incidents that, when looking back with the clear vision of hindsight, you admit to having a conversation with an inoperative third ear?

Here's another example of third-ear listening:

One of my Rutgers IEMBA students approached me at the end of the course last year, frustrated that a few of her classmates were critical of her full engagement in my high-energy-style classes. They questioned whether or not she was being true to her Chinese culture by buying in to a very Western style of presenting and leading. My first instinct was to tell the student how to respond, but instead, I listened and focused on hearing how the criticism had impacted her. Eventually the student discovered her answer in an Eleanor Roosevelt quote I had used that week in class: "No one can make you feel inferior without your consent; someone's opinion of you does not have to become your reality."[4]

When she hit upon the answer, the student brightened, offered a high five, and went back to join her classmates. Now that I've learned to really listen at a higher level, I find that it pays benefits in everything I do, especially in my interactions with those I coach and teach.

## 9 Steps to Third-Ear Listening

I believe our collective lack of listening skills is one of the biggest challenges we all face. Poor listening skills put up roadblocks to your job advancement; poor listening prevents us from having deep and meaningful relationships with our spouses and partners; and, worse, a lack of third-ear listening puts dangerous barriers to keeping peace between nations.

So what can you do to make a change?

First, delete your current approach to listening if you're ready to admit that it's not working for you. Then, apply this nine-step approach that will get you started on the path to "all in" listening:

1. First, make a **vow** to yourself to be a better listener. That's a great start—simple but profound.

2. During conversations, listen for the **content, meaning,** and **feeling** in what the other person is saying. Stop interrupting!

3. Listen to **understand, help, see,** and **support,** not to comment, disagree, and find fault. As Winston Churchill said, "Courage is what it takes to stand up and speak; courage is also what it takes to sit down and listen."[5]

4. Allow moments of **silence** when the person finishes a thought to allow for further comment from the other person. Don't jump in!

5. **Listen** for what the other person is **not saying**.

6. **Refrain** from letting your **past** or your **desire to "fix"** the problem or concern get in the way of hearing the entire message.

7. Ask for **clarification** only when necessary.

8. If the conversation makes you angry or frustrated, keep telling yourself in that moment: "Focus on positive outcomes and expect success!"

9. **BONUS STEP:** Practice these concepts by telling the person you're having a conversation with, to touch your arm every time he or she feels you've checked out of the conversation.

## The Excuse List

Here they are, guiltier than a teenager trying to sneak in the house after curfew, a list of top excuses. (Put check next to the one(s) you can most identify with.)

- ❑ Multitasking.
- ❑ BlackBerrys, cell phones, computers, and the like.
- ❑ Selfishness.
- ❑ Defensiveness.
- ❑ You think you know more than the other person.
- ❑ Difficulty being mentally or emotionally present.
- ❑ Too busy.
- ❑ Cultural difference(s).
- ❑ Payback for how others pay attention to you.
- ❑ Fearful of making this change.
- ❑ Intimidated by the other person (for example, an authority figure).
- ❑ You don't like or disagree with what's being said.

- ❑ Your first instinct is to correct or coach the speaker.
- ❑ You can't help evaluating and/or judging during a conversation.
- ❑ You don't like to hear other people complain.
- ❑ Being empathetic is hard work.

## The Urge Toward Empathy

*"I believe if we lived a life where our mind-set was always, 'How can I make the other person's life better?' we would listen far better than we do,"* Widener University head football coach Isaac Collins shared with me when I asked his philosophy about listening, and in particular today's student athletes. *"I seek to understand and help. We should always be on an out-reach mission. And while we're on that mission we should be extremely humble; humility opens doors. Who is it all about anyway? When we have a mind-set that's totally focused on helping others, listening becomes a lot easier."*

## STOP and START Personal Action Plan

STOP using these typical excuses for not listening with three ears:

- She never listens to me.
- I really don't have time to listen right now. Besides, I don't want everyone else around us to hear our conversation.
- I tried to listen to him before, but he just goes on and on and just repeats himself.
- I get tired of listening to someone who just likes to hear himself talk.

START using these timely exclamations for listening more with three ears:

- Beginning today I will become a better listener.

- I will put together a listening group and practice building my listening muscles.

- I'm going to stop multitasking when someone else is talking.

- I'm going to provide support and empathy and stop trying to fix them.

## START, STOP, CONTINUE DOING Habits

Now that you've given some thought to listening with three ears as a way to rid your life of excuse making, add other **START Doing**, **STOP Doing**, and **CONTINUE Doing** habits that will help you attain this goal:

### I will START Doing:

✓ _____

_____

✓ _____

_____

✓ _____

_____

### I will STOP Doing:

✓ _____

_____

✓ _____

_____

✓ _____

_____

| Continue |

### I will CONTINUE Doing:

✓ _____

_____

✓ _____

_____

✓ _____

_____

## Twitter/Facebook Affirmations

Post or tweet your one key takeaway thought, quote, phrase, or lesson learned in this chapter. Enlist your social network community of friends and colleagues to support your efforts to make positive changes in your life.

Make a note of your Twitter or Facebook post here:

_____

_____

_____

_____

_____

# Winning Way 6

## Remove Self-Created Barriers

*Maybe it's my fault. Maybe I led you to believe it was easy when it wasn't. Maybe I made you think my highlights started at the free throw line, and not in the gym. Maybe I made you think that every shot I took was a game winner. That my game was built on flash, and not fire. Maybe it's my fault that you didn't see that failure gave me strength; that my pain was my motivation. Maybe I led you to believe that basketball was a God-given gift, and not something I worked for...every single day of my life. Maybe I destroyed the game. Or maybe you're just making excuses.*

—Michael Jordan,
NBA Hall of Fame basketball player[1]

Self-created barriers to success and happiness are the most impenetrable. Not only do these barriers belittle us, but they zap our power and ability to take positive action and confidently move forward. If you expect to live an excuse-free life, then *you* must eliminate all the walls *you've* built to protect *you* from perceived pain, disappointment, and rejection.

Sorry, but there's no other way forward. So get busy: start swinging your personal power sledgehammer, and knock down your walls of insecurity, fear, doubt, and pessimism. The clock is ticking, and we've got some life-altering work to do. I know this stuff lives! It's insidious!

There are people in my life who have told me directly, and during workshops, that they will not allow themselves to fall in love, leave their toxic place of employment, and/or put themselves in a position to be judged by others because they don't want to feel the pain or rejection they feel is associated with those endeavors. So they stay in their "caves of life" and retreat to false security with their tired refrain: "I'm not going to even put myself in a position to...."

And, unfortunately, for many of us (perhaps all of us at some level), eliminating the easy ability to use our most practiced excuses of "no," "not now," and "maybe later," creates an even more palpable sense of dread: the fear of success. Just the idea of being accountable for our success rocks us to the core of our being!

Whether you fear that you'll actually be successful at starting you own company, or that returning to school to get a high-demand degree might just result in a high-paying, high-expectations job, or that you'll write a book that someone might actually read and then make the leap of faith and assume that you *really are* an expert at something, or that the love interest of your dreams might just say yes if you asked him or her to meet you for a drink after work, now is the time to just get over it.

It's time to stop choosing barriers and start choosing brighter tomorrows. More importantly, it's time to stop whining and start winning, carving out the life you want (living your life without fear or regret). If you're looking for a place to start reinventing your approach to life and living, then there's no better place to begin. Change this ingrained, comfortable-attitude dynamic, and I guarantee you that your life *will* change in ways you cannot imagine.

*—Barriers Beware Exercise—*

Think about the self-created barriers you've created in the past and how you've struggled to overcome them. Consider also what you believe is really at the root of your self-created barrier (for example, fear and insecurity) and how long the barrier has played a significant role in your life. Once you've given that some thought, imagine what you think your life would be like if that barrier didn't exist.

In the past the main barriers to my success have been:

1. _____
2. _____
3. _____
4. _____
5. _____

I believe the root cause of my self-created barrier include the following:

1. _____
2. _____
3. _____
4. _____
5. _____

My life would be different in the following ways if I did not have these self-created barriers:

1. _____
2. _____
3. _____
4. _____
5. _____

## A Personal Example

Kathy Dempsey (KeepShedding.com) is a good friend and a successful motivational speaker and training/organizational development consultant. A few years before she published her first book, *Shed or You're Dead: 31 unConventional Strategies for Growth & Change*, we were having lunch at her Wilmington, Delaware, home discussing what she saw as her next career move. At the time she was doing very well at her current organization, but she wanted to pursue her dream of being a motivational speaker who focused on helping people deal with change. Because this dream for the future was not a new topic of conversation for us, Kathy knew exactly how I would respond.

"Kath," I said, "you've been saying 'one day' for the past couple of years, but when is *one day* going to be *today*? I know you've heard me say this, but 'one day' is not on the calendar of life. Neither are 'someday,' 'when I get around to it,' 'eventually,' or 'in due time.' When are you going to take your dreams off layaway and turn your resolutions into results?"

I was in full JIMPACT motivational mode!

"When are you going to take off your comfort zone shoes and step into your discomfort zone slippers? You never play it safe in the classroom in front of hundreds of people; why can't you show the same fearlessness outside the classroom? You're talented. Everybody loves you. You've been growing your brand for some time now. When are you going to shed [one of Kathy's motivational words, even then] your training consulting role and do your own thing?"

After I settled back in my seat (and apologized for my motivational rant on her deck), Kathy admitted that she was fearful of losing her *guaranteed* monthly consulting salary.

She liked being able to pay her bills on time and living with security. *"What if things don't go as planned, Jimbo?"* she said. *"I'm not married. I pay all of own my bills. What if I don't get contracts right away? What if I get sick? How am I going to pay for my benefits? What if I go months without work? My savings can only last so far."*

I reminded Kathy that there are no guarantees in life. "You have to start talking yourself into the future you want rather than talking yourself out of it," I told my friend, feeling another motivational blitzkrieg coming on. "You have to coax your success into existence every day by giving your dreams a voice and a choice!" Kathy lasted one more year in her comfortable, safe world of steady paychecks and security before she finally made the leap—and she never looked back.

Kathy's story is a good example of what can happen when we avoid barrier breakdowns, delete limitation language, and decide to unload the heavy, unbearable baggage of fear—to shed it, as Kathy would say. Life has no safety net or guaranteed solutions. You take a risk every time you open your front door or walk down the street or ride your bike on a Sunday afternoon or drive your car to the grocery store or board a plane for a quick business trip or get on a cruise ship bound for Italy. If the path to having the life we want was easy, then that would be one crowded road!

However, most of us allow that small, self-critical voice in our head to hold sway over our future. We allow our past to control our future. We allow our fear of being judged, evaluated, or rejected talk us into slamming the door on opportunity and padlocking it shut. Worse, we allow the fear that we'll actually be successful to trump all options so that we can stay in our safe, predictable, and, sadly, mediocre world. My friend Kathy was able to get past her success gatekeepers, and I believe you can do it, too.

## Taking Your Own Advice

Perhaps one of the reasons I got so motivated cheering my friend Kathy on to start her own business was the fact that I had been in her position rationalizing and making excuses why I should *not* go out on my own.

Sure, it was easy to think, *"I'm going to be up there one day!"* when I heard an excellent speaker give a powerful message that touched and motivated me. But soon my energy would wane, and my vision would fade and be replaced with the more familiar and limiting answers, such as *"So what am I going to do? Just quit my job? Who are you kidding?"* I fought these thoughts, Ali versus Frazier style, until I developed a simple way for dealing with them. Every time one of those dream-killing thoughts tried to sneak into my mind, I said in my head or out loud (and meant it), "I'll show you; it's my time!"

Eventually, I began to believe that it really *was* my time, and I took action to make it happen. I know that seems like a simplistic, positive psychology answer, but it worked. I'll take positive affirmations mixed with great expectations, faith, and a clear vision over "what if?" conversations any day of the week. We all have baggage, complicated commitments, and obligations, and we all know nothing is simple, but eventually we all end up standing outside a door we know leads to a different life—the life we want—and a decision must be made: Are we going to open the door, or walk away and return to the not-quite-satisfying life we know?

I heard hundreds of clients and training workshop participants voice the same dilemma during the years I worked as an organizational development consultant and during my time working in Corporate America. I heard every variety of excuse in cafeterias, in elevators, before and after meetings, in hallways, on planes while traveling, at happy hour networking events, and on the fields and courts at intramural sports. The unifying theme was predictable: Many people wished that they were doing something other than what they were currently doing. Yet all had (for one reason or another) chosen to stay, regardless of the mental or emotional anguish they were experiencing. (Winning Way 7 continues this theme. We'll discuss more about pursuing your passion and not a paycheck.) As the saying goes, I wish I had a nickel every time I heard someone say, "Can't wait until the weekend gets here" or "This place drives me nuts," or "Same stuff, different day." What was most rare was this simple statement: "I love what I'm doing."

Even with an enthusiastic, live-your-life-out-loud coach to tell them it was okay to make a decision, most of the time I heard "but" or "what if?" replies to every empowering suggestion I offered. Most of these individuals had simply developed a "this is all that I have, and I can have no more" mindset. Yes, some worked for obnoxious leaders or managers and had legitimate complaints. Others were confronted with situations beyond their control that made immediate change appear impossible, but that does not excuse everyone. For the vast majority of us, it is possible to change. And it starts with you deciding to break down the walls and barriers!

## Egregious 8 Barriers

I've assembled the "Egregious 8" self-created barriers that I most often hear. If any of these are close to the mark for you, then go to *www.noexcuseguide.com* for solid advice on how to successfully confront and conquer your own self-created barriers:

1.  I don't want to be judged by others.

2.  I tried it before and it didn't work.

3. The odds are against me.

4. I let other people's opinion of me become my reality.

5. I know someone who tried it before, and he or she failed.

6. I've talked myself into believing that it's not for me.

7. I've talked myself into believing that I can do without it.

8. I've determined that the timing is bad right now for me to do it.

One caveat to all this "you can do it" advice: Those who decide to shed their self-created barriers do not always find immediate success or hit the jackpot. But that's hardly the point. Simply taking action is an end in itself, and leads to new paths and different ways to succeed and move forward. You can't really lose. So go ahead—put in a few coins and pull the lever. You might win the jackpot. Rather than 7-7-7 appearing on your screen, you get: Joy! Joy! Joy!

## Promises, Promises

When I started JIMPACT, I was full of "can't fail" enthusiasm. The notion that I was truly living my dream was infatuating. I had worked my network and received commitments from a number of colleagues who said they would help me find work. For one reason or another, that work didn't materialize, and so my first year as founder, owner, and CEO of JIMPACT Enterprises was extremely humbling, but character-building. My income went from six figures to six prayers a day that I would steer this wayward ship in the appropriate direction. I eventually righted the ship, but it certainly tested my commitment to the power of positive thinking and energy.

Still, my story of struggle is not that unique. Sardek Love is a friend of mine who travels the world consulting for Fortune 100 companies. Sardek's current reality is a lot different than the one he had just a few years ago as he navigated his way through a series of poisonous corporate cultures as he did his best to play along and follow traditional office politics guidelines.

Unfortunately, even this extremely bright and dedicated employee—despite his best efforts—ended up in the human resources office handing over his company ID and office key. *"It was a shocking experience,"* Sardek says, but he decided to see the setback as an opportunity. *"At my last job, to say that I was thrown under the bus would be an understatement. I got fired. No job. No benefits. No severance. Nevertheless, to this day I say that I was **fired to success**. No 'woe is me.' No pity party. No 'I can't do this.' I moved on and up."*

Sardek said that within 15 minutes after being fired, a friend called from another organization and offered him his first consulting gig. So in 2006, he started his own company, Infinity Consulting and Training Solutions. He helps organizations around the world—the Caribbean, West Africa, Europe, Southeast Asia, Asia, Asia Pacific, and the Middle East—maximize profitability in a global economy.

Here's what Sardek has to say about facing and overcoming adversity without excuses. He posted a slightly different version on his Facebook page, shortly after I interviewed him:

1.  *Believe you will get through it and things will get better. Everything starts and ends in your belief about any and every situation.*

2. *Control your thoughts and eliminate any thoughts that can limit your success.*

3. *Be clear about what you want and, more importantly, be clear about what you don't want. Make your focus, though, what you do want. This helps you act your way to success.*

4. *Rely on your SUCCESS TEAM. Rather than facing it alone, find a small group of people you trust to help you defeat the challenging situation.*

5. *Focus on getting better by not repeating the behaviors that created the adversity.*

6. *Put yourself in winning situations and avoid temptations that will derail your success at beating the adverse conditions you're facing.*

In order to move beyond our self-created barriers, we have to get our thoughts and beliefs in alignment. Remember: How you feel influences how you behave or perform. As my friend, mentor, Mike Jones says, *"Energy and action follow thought—that life only has the meaning that you give it—that everything you fight against weakens you—and that you should have the dream, then wake up...the dream is only the first step."*

## Just Get Past Your Barriers

My job makes me privy to many inspiring, "ignore our barriers" stories and testimonials. I'm sure you've had similar experiences of being amazed as someone recounts harrowing, even life-threatening experiences that required strength and resolve that you might not think you possess. I am here to tell you that you do—in fact, we all do—if we're just willing to be open to the possibility.

Here's how Karen Cheng, one of my Rutgers IEMBA Singapore students, summed up the lessons learned from her struggle to overcome a rare, chronic auto-immune muscle disease that left the once–deep-sea diving, mountain-climbing, and skydiving enthusiast nearly immobile (unable, as she shared with me, to successfully use toilet paper when the time called):

> *Mahatma Ghandhi once said, "Live as if you were to die tomorrow. Learn as if you were to live forever."[2] I have learned something new every day and never does a day go by without my reflecting on what was new that day. I do not have time nor do I know how to be bored. Boredom should be banished; it has no place in our society today. I make it a point to seek new experiences and to challenge old ones. I will not place any barriers on myself. Waking up every day and being able to actually get out of bed is a true blessing. One that I never take for granted.*

Remember: Circumstances don't make or break you; they reveal who you are!

## STOP and START Personal Action Plan

STOP using these typical excuses for not removing your personal barriers:

- I'm fine with the way things are now.
- It doesn't make a difference what I do.
- I am this way because of how I was raised.
- I have bills to pay; I can't risk losing my job.

START using these timely exclamations for removing your personal barriers:

- My best is yet to come!
- My life only has the meaning that I give it!
- I'm sick and tired of being sick and tired!
- I can't savor my moments if I'm not creating them. It's time for me to start creating!

### START, STOP, CONTINUE DOING Habits

Now that you've given some thought to removing your personal barriers as a way to rid your life of excuse making, add other **START Doing**, **STOP Doing**, and **CONTINUE Doing** habits that will help you attain this goal:

**I will START Doing:**

✓ _____

✓ _____

✓ _____

**I will STOP Doing:**

✓ _____

✓ _____

✓ _____

Continue

## I will CONTINUE Doing:

✓ _____

_____

✓ _____

_____

✓ _____

_____

## Twitter/Facebook Affirmations

Post or tweet your one key takeaway thought, quote, phrase, or lesson learned in this chapter. Enlist your social network community of friends and colleagues to support your efforts to make positive changes in your life.

Make a note of your Twitter or Facebook post here:

_____

_____

_____

_____

_____

# Winning Way 7

## Pursue Your Passion, Not a Paycheck

*Above all, be true to yourself, and if you cannot put your heart in it, take yourself out of it.*
—Hardy D. Jackson, author[1]

Asking if you are currently pursuing your life's passion might seem a naive question just as the nation emerges from its worst economic crisis since the Great Depression. Or perhaps it's the absolute best time to give this question some serious thought. To begin, here are a few questions I'd like you to think about:

- Are you pursuing your passion, or are you pursuing a paycheck?

- Is your career moving in the direction you want?

- Are you using the same predictable life script you've always used?

- Have you been doing the same thing at the same place for as long as you can remember?

- Do you think to yourself most days: *"How did I end up here?"*

- Are you working for someone who absolutely drives you crazy? Do you fantasize various scenarios involving your boss, manager, or supervisor that put you in a position of power so that *you* are able to demonstrate to everyone what a despicable human being he or she really is and why all the complaining and whining you've been doing is justified?

If any of these scenarios are familiar, you can take some cold comfort that you are not alone—by a long shot!

## Why We Don't Like Our Jobs

A recent Gallup study on job dissatisfaction suggests that only 29 percent of the U.S. workforce is actively engaged with their jobs (54 percent say they are not engaged, and 17 percent say they are actively disengaged). So the numbers are telling us this: More than 70 percent of us are just going through the motions at work, still looking to get paid 100 percent, and, even worse for organizations, actively at odds with our organizations.[2] The reasons for this disengagement are myriad, but, according to a January 2010 CBS News poll, the most commonly cited reasons for our checking out from our jobs include the following:[3]

- Uninteresting job.
- Incomes have not kept up with inflation.
- Soaring healthcare costs that have cut workers' take-home pay.
- Little to no teamwork.
- No job security.
- Dislike of coworkers.
- Difficult commute to work.
- Poor overall communications at work.
- Dislike or poor relationship with manager.

Need more reasons why we say we don't like our jobs? Here's what a March 16, 2011, article in *Small Business Trends* magazine listed as top job dissatisfaction complaints for workers:[4]

- Low pay.
- Little to no career advancement.
- Lack of opportunities.

In addition to discussing what workers didn't like about their jobs, the article also listed what the surveyed workers would like to see more of in their jobs and from their organizations. It is interesting to note that 40 percent of the workers under the age of 25 were the most fed up with their organizations, with workers between 25 and 34 years old coming in a close second on the dissatisfaction scale. Here's what the article said these workers wanted:[5]

- New, challenging assignments.
- Flexible work arrangements.
- Access to more leadership positions within their companies.

## What Are You Going to Do?

Of course, this research is probably not telling you anything you don't know or likely haven't experienced firsthand. My question is this: *What are you going to do about it?* Wait for them to change? If you're honest about it, your choices are pretty limited once all the "why not?" noise is filtered out. You can continue to put up with it and be miserable, or you can determine to seek a new path for yourself—to seek *joy* and not just another *job*. You must really stand before the harsh light of that clothing store (or bathroom) mirror and engage in some serious self-interrogation. Why do you:

- Spend eight-plus hours each day in a job you loathe?

- Keep reporting into a boss who shows disrespect if not downright contempt for your work no matter how hard you try?

- Keep pursuing someone else's dream for you and not your own?

- Hide your creativity and your unique God-given talents? Why don't you let them shine and be recognized?

- Continue to travel so far, round-trip, to a place that doesn't appreciate the value that you bring each day?

- Continue to believe that your current job is the only job in the world for you?

- Continue to put yourself in a position each day to spend at least a third of your day with people who are just as fed up as you are and who want to see you fail?

These are tough questions to answer honestly without the crutch of excuses to deflect the blame toward someone else. Your boss, the economy, and the possibility of failure (and, more frightening, the possibility of success) are just convenient smoke screens for the real culprit behind your inertia. Only you can make the necessary changes that will ultimately impact your situation at work and in life. Only you can determine that today's the day you're going to say, "I've had enough!" and make your life work the way you want it to!

Imagine (if you want to hum the Beatles' classic, you can as you read on) a workplace in which everyone pursued their passion instead of a just a paycheck. Imagine the energy, enthusiasm, trust, and empowerment that would exist.

Imagine no more sulking, sour attitudes, and tantrums, and instead workers heading to work smiling and looking forward to their jobs, free from stress and worry. Here's something else hard to imagine: people looking forward to their performance appraisal meetings with their managers.

In this fantasy world, you would work late on occasion because you want to, not out of fear you'd be caught unprepared and shamed or, worse, fired. Your boss might even be supportive of your decision to leave the department to acquire new skills or even leave the organization so that you could pursue your dreams to start your own business. Your occasional happy hour discussions with your colleagues would be all positive and uplifting about work, and would never degenerate into pity parties about terrible bosses, managers, and organizations.

Of course, none of us are holding our breath for such a renaissance of the workplace to occur. That's why you're reading this book. You're not willing to wait for such an unlikely change to happen. Instead, you're actively looking to create this reality for yourself.

## Pursuing Your Passion

Dr. Brene Brown, research professor at the University of Houston Graduate School of Social Work, studies wholeheartedness and vulnerability, and really gets it when it comes to why some purse their passion while others pursue a paycheck. From reading a number of her articles and watching her various interviews, I've determined that she, too, believes it's all about focus and perspective, and that unfortunately many of us see more potholes than we see possibilities. Dr. Brown believes that many of us want guarantees that "it's going to work," to move forward. Wouldn't that be nice? So we stay stuck. We listen to others who share their "play it safe stories" and remain in the bad marriage (in other words, job) until death do we part.

When did we start believing that we weren't good enough or talented enough to pursue our passion? Did I miss the memo—I mean, e-mail (oops, I'm a Baby Boomer)? When did we start letting what "they" said become our reality. Why do we always listen to "them"? "They" and "them" are passion killers, and there are many of "them" in our society.

Feeling feisty last week, I posted this as my Facebook status update:

> *How many people have told you—you need to write a book? How many have said to you—you need to start your own company? How many people have said to you—you do this or that better than anyone that they know. How many more people are you waiting to hear from until you DO IT? How many more years have to go by before you DO IT? Take your talents out of the waiting room. Stop sitting on your stories. Take your poems out of prison. C'mon...is life in your comfort zone working for you that well?*

Dr. Brown agrees with my "play full out philosophy." I'm certain that she would delete the "they/them" file if she had one. We cannot let perceived disappointment be our roadblocks. Being a vulnerability expert, of course, she champions that we should be more vulnerable. It's a shame that so many of us look at vulnerability as a weakness. Actually, it's a strength!

Vulnerability adds to our power, faith, creativity, and authenticity and helps us to connect with people—and pursue our passion. And isn't that what it's all about?

My close friend and business partner, Raimond Honig (a successful entrepreneur who has started and run 12 companies in the Netherlands), echoes these sentiments on what it takes to move beyond the attitude boundaries that trap many of us in lives we don't want. He is also an awesome example of someone who fearlessly moves past supposed boundaries with positive thinking. In fact, his signature entrepreneurial wisdom is encapsulated in his belief that "if it is to be, it's up to me."

Raimond grew up in a poor but very loving family as the youngest of seven children. *"We didn't have much—no car, small house, and couldn't afford to celebrate the holidays like most other people,"* he says. *"I grew up wanting to be somebody special and successful when I got older. As a result, I developed a pretty strong work ethic. My dad used to say that if you weren't smart you had to work extremely hard. To that end, if you told me I couldn't do it or that I wasn't going to be successful at it, like my dad used to do a lot, my mind-set was that I'll show you."*

Raimond says that his father's pessimistic outlook on his son's potential for success helped him build a strong work ethic early in his life. *"In addition to going to school every day, I started working when I was 11 delivering up to 800 newspapers a day,"* he said. *"It took me and my 11-year-old muscles approximately four hours to deliver those newspapers. I think I made about ten dollars a week."*

Throughout his teen years, Raimond worked at a number of jobs, taking advantage of everything he could learn, whether the job was working in a restaurant or working at a swim club. He also excelled at sports (especially in tae kwon do and kickboxing) and eventually became the Dutch champion and the German champion. He finished third in the World Championships in 1992.

*"In most of my jobs I moved and thought faster than many of my bosses. I always wanted to move up because I*

wasn't content," Raimond said. *"At 25, I decided it would be better to start my own company* [Bureau Honig and Partners]. *In three years the company grew from two people to 100. Since then, I've owned a couple of other companies* [including the one he was in negotiations to sell this year, Credit Management Institute BV; if the sale goes through he will become one of their senior leaders] *and I've been pretty successful in my career. Still I wasn't happy."* So in characteristic, "if it's to be, it's up to me" fashion, Raimond made a change.

As he entered his forties, Raimond has switched gears and life focus toward the things that really make him happy, including spending time with his family:

*I've shifted my focus to my passion, which is connecting with people, not obtaining things. I just love connecting with people all over the world. I've learned to be honest with myself and therefore to be honest with others. You have to ask yourself if your energy and spirit* [are] *negatively impacting the people around you and your environment. You do not have to turn off someone else's light to make yours shine. Life is too short. You have to ask yourself if all of the stuff you have and the debt you've acquired is really worth it.*

From his perspective on the other side of making a big change in his life, Raimond offers this advice: *"Spend your time doing what you love and connecting with yourself and with others."* At the end of the day, he says, that connection is all that matters.

## What Success Means

We have all heard the excellent, but hard to implement, advice such as "just do what you love and success will follow." Here are a few other success nuggets:

"The ONLY way you can find a meaningful, fulfilling life is by performing work that engages your heart and mind."

—Arthur Miller (People Management International, LLC)[6]

"Success in the knowledge economy comes to those who know themselves, their strengths, their values and how they best perform."

—Peter Drucker[7]

## Don't Settle for Tolerable

Unfortunately, most of us don't have a clear understanding of what that elusive "love" is, so we settle for something we "like" or, worse, something we tolerate. That last state of being—tolerating our work—is not going to take you far in today's competitive job market. Plus it's going to make you miserable. No employer can afford to pay employees who are so disengaged with their work. Employers are demanding more engagement (passion) from their employees. It's not just the economic conditions driving employers to favor fully engaged employees. Employers have learned by experience that engaged employees are productive employees, no matter the state of the economy.

How do you determine your calling and tap into your own reservoir of engagement, energy, and passion? How do you stop making excuses for why you are still tolerating your life and career? I've done a lot of career coaching and have heard many of my clients lament that despite being grown up, they had not identified their life's calling. Many moved into a career that was expected of them or took a career path based on job prospects, not on the career they originally mapped out or imagined. So, how do you reverse course, or make a radical change in your life to pursue goals more aligned with your passion and purpose?

According to Maryls Hanson, MS, and Merle Hanson, PhD, authors of the book, *Passion and Purpose: How to Identify and Leverage the Powerful Patterns that Shape Your Work/Life*, the answer is already inside us waiting to be discovered. The book points out:

> Our passion and our purpose are already with us, waiting to be discovered, if we will just take the time to examine our lives and our work. Once we have these insights about ourselves, we must acknowledge their enduring nature. We are not made of putty, waiting to be shaped into whatever the world wants or needs. Each of us possesses a pattern that orients and directs our behavior; it also defines what will be meaningful and fulfilling in our lives. The evidence of this pattern has shown through our entire lives. We need to take the time to identify, understand and act on it.[8]

The work of finding your own passion, as described by Maryls and Merle Hanson, is "the essential ingredient for a successful life" and is what eventually provides meaning:

> There is nothing neutral about our passions and our purpose. Either we respond to what these powerful forces present to us in our daily lives and in our fantasies, or we suffer from the neglect of ourselves.... We need work that is more than a livelihood. We need work that is life itself. We need to listen to our passions and let them help us define our purpose and shape our work/life. It is only through this process that we find significant value in ourselves and thus build our feelings of self-worth.[9]

# Finding Your Passion

As you might guess, finding the one thing that really engages and inspires you will require some work. It's a process that needs a beginning in order to have an end point. So, if you're ready to commit to the process, then let's begin.

First, grab a pen to jot down your thoughts and ideas as you work through the Passion and Purpose Discovery Exercise (adapted from *Passion and Purpose* by Marlys Hanson and Merle Hanson) to uncover what you enjoy doing and what you find satisfying and to uncover if you are currently passionlessly employed.

## —*Passion and Purpose Discovery Exercise*[10]—

Read the following statements and jot down your reactions to each one. For some, your initial answer might be a simple "yes," whereas other statements may prompt a longer response. Feel free to answer in this book, on a separate sheet of paper, or on your computer or tablet device. You can also go to *www.noexcuseguide.com.*

- It takes you longer to accomplish the work than it takes some of your colleagues who seem to be a better "fit." Yes ___ No ___

- The performance of the work takes on a "hollow" quality; you start performing without thinking too much about what you are doing. Yes ___ No ___

- You find yourself making errors that seem minor and unimportant to you, but others seem to have a different reaction. Yes ___ No ___

- You have trouble getting up in the morning and hate to think about another day (week, month, year) of work ahead. Yes ___ No ___

- You are absent from work more frequently and you are ill more often. Yes ___ No ___

- You rarely read about, discuss, or explore the content of your work on your personal time. Yes ___ No ___

- You are less likely to speak up in meetings, to engage in discussion and debate with colleagues, to take on additional involvement in related tasks, or to offer leadership. Yes ___ No ___

- You are becoming more involved with interpersonal difficulties at work and in your other relationships. You find yourself blaming others for things they are doing or not doing. Yes ___ No ___

- Your self-esteem diminishes because you are not being recognized and rewarded for who you are. Indeed, your image may become tarnished as you are viewed performing work/ roles that do not engage your passion and thus your best energy and effort. Yes ___ No ___

- Your overall health is suffering. Your headaches are more frequent and more severe. Your blood pressure has increased. Yes ___ No ___

- You are becoming more impatient, argumentative, and moody. Yes ___ No ___

- You appear energy-less and lethargic; people are always asking you what's wrong. Yes ___ No ___

- You begin spending more time on your computer, at work, on non-work-related sites. Yes ___ No ___

- You're one of the last to arrive in the morning and one of the first to leave in the afternoon. Yes ___ No ___

- Nothing about the job excites you anymore. Yes ___ No ___

- You begin to leave the office each day not having accomplished anything of significance. Yes ___ No ___

- You offer excuses for your situation, typically blaming your manager and your company. Yes ___ No ___

## What Are Your Motivational Patterns?

Now let's see if we can uncover what you're passionate about as well as your Motivational Patterns are. According to the Hansons, "When you understand precisely how your Motivational Pattern impacts your performance and fulfillment, you will have the foundation for meaningful career discussions and joint planning with supervision."[11]

These authors believe that the comprehensive, analytic process of identifying your Motivational Pattern will prepare you to describe, in specific detail, the nature of your work-related passions and the purpose of your efforts. By using this methodology, you will also be able to recognize the limitations of preference-based career inventories that you may have taken in high school or college, or even as part of a job-search or career-development process.

The Motivational Pattern is based on specific evidence of recurring behavior from lifelong enjoyable and satisfying experiences. For me, growing up and throughout my education and early employment, I had a number of achievement experiences that involved audiences and listeners in some way, so I developed my own recurring evidence metric connected to seeking out and practicing my passion and purpose. Even when my jobs did not require it, I still found a way to make presentations.

## Finding the Source of Your Passion

The Hansons believe that, because we develop the evidence, the process becomes somewhat like holding a mirror up to your life and looking for the recurring themes that are unique to you. Let's assess your self-understanding of your passions and purpose by considering a number of questions relative to the presence/absence of critical motivations.

The questions that follow, adapted from *Passion and Purpose* by Marlys Hanson and Merle Hanson, address factors that contribute significantly to performance success (or failure), as well as to personal satisfaction from performing a given role. By thoughtfully completing this exercise, you can determine if you need to dig deeper to uncover more understanding about your Motivational Patterns or if you're more equipped to pursue your passions.

This exercise should help you clarify what motivates you. (For these questions, "motivated" means that this is an activity that you both enjoy doing and feel you do well). As you're responding to each item, think about situations that provide "evidence" for your response.

- Do you know what it takes to get you started and actively interested in pursuing a task or activity? Yes ___ No ___
- Are you "motivated" to sell? Yes ___ No ___
- Are you "motivated" to plan? Yes ___ No ___

- Can you identify three subjects that interest you? Yes ___ No ___

- Do you know whether or not you're at home in a politically charged environment? Yes ___ No ___

- Are you aware of how you would react to do a job that was not well defined in terms of what you were expected to accomplish? Yes ___ No ___

- Do you require ample time to prepare when asked to respond to an unexpected request? Yes ___ No ___

- Do you know whether you must have a standard or other way of measuring performance? Yes ___ No ___

- Is exercising initiative a high priority for you? Yes ___ No ___

- Would you say you know how much and what kind of stress and pressure you can handle comfortably? Yes ___ No ___

- Do you have entrepreneurial tendencies? Yes ___ No ___

- Do you have specific goals? Yes ___ No ___ If not, do you know why? Yes ___ No ___

- Are you a person who recognizes an opportunity before it is apparent to others? Yes ___ No ___

- Is money important to you? Yes ___ No ___

- Are you a conceptual person? Yes ___ No ___

- Are you a creative person? Yes ___ No ___

- Are you a strategic person? Yes ___ No ___

- Are you "motivated" to make risky decisions when your reputation is on the line? Yes ___ No ___

- Are you comfortable confronting others? Yes ___ No ___

- Are you aware of the reasons why you lose your cool (when you do)? Yes ___ No ___

- Do you know why you get depressed occasionally? Yes ___ No ___

- Are you a leader? Yes ___ No ___

- Are you "motivated" to build relationships with others? Yes ___ No ___

- Do you sweat the details? Yes ___ No ___

- Are you good at probing others for information? Yes ___ No ___

- Are you good at problem-solving? Yes ___ No ___

- Are you a results-oriented person? Yes ___ No ___

- Are you someone who could be trusted to get the job done, in spite of the difficulties? Yes ___ No ___

- Do you like working with people? Yes ___ No ___

- Do you like working in teams? Yes ___ No ___

- Do you like to travel for work? Yes ___ No ___

- Do you prefer to work alone? Yes ___ No ___

- Can you see how something will look in advance of it being made a reality? Yes ___ No ___

- Do you like to go beyond where other people are? Yes ___ No ___

- Do you worry about the bottom line? Yes ___ No ___

- If you have management ability, could you describe how you get things done through others? Yes ___ No ___
- Are you "motivated" to teach? Yes ___ No ___
- Are you good at making presentations/facilitating workshops? Yes ___ No ___
- If yes, do you know what kinds of people and learning situations you find agreeable? Yes ___ No ___
- Can you define what it is that you want to accomplish in your work—more than anything else? Yes ___ No ___

If you were not able to provide a clear "yes" or "no" answer to all of the questions, that's all right. You have still succeeded in creating a blueprint to begin the process of more fully appreciating the possible potential in understanding and utilizing your innate motivations (both personally and professionally).

You will find more about utilizing your Motivational Patterns at *www.noexcuseguide.com*, along with additional ways to move past tired excuses and toward finding your true passion and purpose in life.

## Your Challenge

It's time to throw away your scripts and break up your "safe stuff, different day" routine. You're on the clock. Organizations will always have (or create) positions for people who bring immense value. Passionate people bring value. You have it in you. You already know how to pursue a paycheck (and how's that working for you?). Unleash and unlock your potential, and I guarantee you'll never be the same!

## STOP and START Personal Action Plan

STOP using these typical excuses for not pursuing your passion and purpose:

- There aren't any other jobs out there.
- Companies don't really allow you to perform outside the box.
- I have too many bills to pay.
- In this difficult economy I'm just glad to have a job.

START using these timely exclamations for pursuing your passion and purpose:

- I've been sitting on my potential for too long. I'm going to pursue my passion!
- Life is too short to sit around and wait for things to happen!
- I have to live my life!
- Money doesn't buy happiness the way passion does! Show me the passion!

## START, STOP, CONTINUE DOING Habits

Now that you've given some thought to pursuing your passion and purpose and not just a paycheck as a way to rid your life of excuse making, add other **START Doing, STOP Doing,** and **CONTINUE Doing** habits that will help you attain this goal.

### I will START Doing:

✓ _____

✓ _____
_____

✓ _____
_____

### I will STOP Doing:

✓ _____
_____

✓ _____
_____

✓ _____
_____

### I will CONTINUE Doing:

✓ _____

✓ _____
_____

✓ _____
_____

## Twitter/Facebook Affirmations

Post or tweet your one key takeaway thought, quote, phrase, or lesson learned in this chapter. Enlist your social network community of friends and colleagues to support your efforts to make positive changes in your life.

Make a note of your Twitter or Facebook post here:

_____

_____

_____

_____

_____

# Winning Way 8

## Give Up "Right-Fighting"

*What is your primary concern here, to have the pride of
being right or the joy of being loved?*
—Kevin FitzMaurice, author, writer, and
mental-health and spiritual counselor[1]

When was the last time you were in a "right-fight"? You
know—one of those conversations (arguments, more often
than not) that you somehow allow to devolve into a high-
stakes, fight-to-the-death opinion battle. If you happen to
have a serious right-fight predilection, then my guess is that
you've likely suited up to do battle with a wide range of people, including coworkers, friends, family members, airport
check-in or gate staff, store clerks, and almost anyone else
who happens to challenge your "rightness" on a wide variety
of subjects. If you happen to be one of these chronic right-
fight warriors or even if you're more of an occasional right-
fighter, here are some questions I'd like you to ponder:

- Why is it so important for you to be right?
- Why can't you just "let it go" and move on?
- Why is making your point so important that it
  overshadows everything else?

Having trouble answering these questions honestly?
Don't worry; this chapter provides the needed insight to
stop this insidious and destructive habit. As you will learn,

not only does right-fighting destroy relationships, but it also stands squarely in the way of your quest to live an excuse-free life. This chapter peels back the underlying causes of your right-fighting disease and exposes an underlying fact that many of us find hard to accept: It's okay to have a strong point of view, but it is *not* okay to *insist* that others share your same view.

## A Personal Example

Even if you are not a habitual right-fighter, it's a pretty safe bet to assume that you and your spouse or partner occasionally engage in a few right-fight confrontations. I know—it seems to go with the territory. As your experience tells you, these battles do not have to be about anything significant—for example, not following through on a simple household assignment or even leaving toothpaste in the sink in the morning. Somehow, being right takes on unimagined importance and there you are, and for no good reason, completely out of control insisting that your significant other is absolutely, irrevocably wrong!

My wife and I came within striking distance of such an argument recently while driving to Philadelphia to pick up our daughter Lauren for the weekend. When her schedule allows (not often enough) she is our designated babysitter. What made this narrowly avoided confrontation so significant was the fact that the conversation began with an off-hand remark about the nature of forgiveness. I had read an interesting article about the topic and was passing it along, mainly just to pass the time. I didn't really have a hidden agenda (I promise!).

Before I knew it, our conversation was escalating toward the outer bounds of right-fighting. I could see the train wreck of a conversation, but was at first powerless to control where my offhand remark was taking us. Soon, my wife's voice started getting edgy (as did mine), and we started making our points louder and with more certainty and conviction.

At some point I could see that our conversation had reached a crossroads. I knew I had a choice. I could sense that my wife was getting annoyed with me. Did I want to be right, or did I want to stop arguing my point and enjoy the rest of my day? I thought to myself, *"Do I want to move on or spend the rest of the day, and probably the evening, participating in a battle of high stakes 'silent treatment'?"* As much as I wanted to get my last points in (to convince her that my way was the right way), I let it go. And even though my wife was still making her closing argument five minutes later, I had emotionally moved on. I didn't want to be right anymore. I knew that this was a no-win situation, and ultimately it was a silly and unproductive way to spend our time together. I made a choice to walk away.

## Is Being Right Important to You?

How important is it for *you* to be right? Why do we have this right-fighting desire? (I disagree with the notion that it's a need.) Is it our desire to be in control? Is it our ego? Is it insecurity? Do we pursue being right for recognition or approval? Does always being right make us feel superior, smart, or worthy? Whatever the reason, we all are guilty of the annoying practice.

My opinion is that right-fighting has nothing to do with a dictionary definition of the word *right*: "in conformity with fact, reason, truth or some standard or principle; correct; correct in judgment, opinion or action."[2] Instead, for most people my guess is that right-fighting has more to do with having an agenda than getting the facts straight! But, then, perhaps that's my own agenda showing.

## Who Wins in a Right-Fight?

"Let go of your attachment to being right, and suddenly your mind is more open. You're able to benefit from the unique viewpoints of others, without being crippled by your own judgment."

—Ralph Marston, The Daily Motivator[3]

Who really wins when you're right? Writer and mental-health and spiritual counselor Kevin FitzMaurice offers probing questions and reflections about our tendency to insist upon our rightness on his Website.[4] Here's my take—an edited version of Kevin's questions and reflections:

- Are you so sensitive that you cannot stand to have anyone think different from you?
- Diversity, perspective, and variation are a part of life.
- Do you really want to relate only to people who see life, live life, and think about life exactly the way you do?
- I have to be true to my experience and so do you. What is the value in arguing whose experience is right?
- Please listen to my entire message. I promise to do the same for you.
- You are wasting my time, energy, and breath when you argue about memories of a sitation, because we all have our own map.
- What is more important to you: my feelings or your ego?
- Facts or feelings—what's more important to you? When you choose my feelings, I feel loved, valued, and appreciated.

- You cannot force your life or your stories into someone else's reality. He or she will not experience like you.

## The Emotional Cost of Right-Fighting

Right-fighting certainly leaks into other aspects of our lives, and I believe that right-fighting harms loving relationships. In the midst of a marital tussle, whether brief or lengthy, no one is seeking to understand; both are seeking to be understood and to be right. If it's a brief, "drive-by" right-fight, the spouse on the receiving end is emotionally wounded, in pain, and left wondering where that outburst came from. At some level, though upset because he or she wanted to do the same thing but opted to keep his or her mouth shut to keep the peace, this spouse knows that if he or she spoke up now, it would flare into a "tit-for-tat" right-fight.

If it's a lengthy quarrel, the right-fighting eventually turns into an argument on the rules of right-fighting (who speaks first, when you can butt in, how many points the person can make before you get to respond, and so on) and the initial arguing point is loss. Everyone loses, even if you win. What's also lost during these battles is the fact that people change only when they choose to change, not because you provide a litany of what you think are sound reasons. What's the result? Dislike builds up. Frustration lingers. Animosity swells, and two people who once vowed to take care of and love each other until death do they part, become unofficial roommates who walk around on eggshells avoiding the start of another right-fight.

Most of us will admit to some level of right-fighting if challenged, but for most of us this reasonable, reflective side is soon overshadowed by an overwhelming desire to defend our position or decision. Here's an example from my trainer, speaker, facilitator JIMPACT BOOT CAMP:

### In the "Hot Seat"

Participants at these workshops make a presentation to the entire group and then sit in the "hot seat" in front of their peers for feedback. The group provides both praise (what the presenter did well) and polish (what the presenter could have done better). When I first used this exercise in my classes, participants were allowed to respond to the feedback they received while in the hot seat. Unfortunately, many participants took this as an opportunity to "explain" their approach or presentation decisions. Now these sessions are governed by a different rule: The person receiving the feedback cannot speak unless it's to ask the person giving the feedback to speak louder or to clarify a point. He or she can also say "thank you," but that's it.

I had to make this change because these exercises often became prime examples of right-fighting and ultimate excuse making! Instead of taking the feedback as an opportunity to learn, participants used this opportunity to communicate as a license to argue for their rightness. How can you learn if you're not really listening to the insight others have to offer? Ego stymies personal growth every time.

In addition to weakening your relationships, the desire to be right has the awful consequence of changing how people perceive you and determines how you will live your life. A "that's my story and I'm sticking to it" attitude drives people away, because they see you as arrogant, self-righteous, aloof, and sanctimonious.

## Right-Fighting Checklist

Are you a frequent right-fighter? Not sure? Here's a 21-point checklist along with an action plan to make positive changes. I suggest you go to *www.noexcuseguide.com* and print out the worksheet. Post it on your wall or another visible place, and start correcting these destructive behaviors. As a right-fighter, do you:

1. Reject, dismiss, and ignore others' ideas or offers to help?
2. Take things way too personally, way too often?
3. Become defensive quickly?
4. Have people accuse you of being selfish?
5. Have people say to you: "You always have to be right?"
6. Believe that everyone has something against you?
7. Play the victim role?
8. Criticize, criticize, and criticize?
9. Become angry and annoyed very fast?
10. Frequently use sarcasm regarding the quality of others' ideas?
11. Blame, judge, and make fun of people?
12. Seldom believe, during the disagreement, that you may be wrong?
13. Seldom take the high road?
14. Fight even stronger depending on how important you perceive the stakes are?

15. Tend not to have many friends or close relationships?

16. Justify, defend, and rationalize your behaviors?

17. See the right-fight in others but not in yourself?

18. Think you're misunderstood?

19. Have a difficult time listening?

20. Seldom accept personal responsibility and account-ability for what happens after the right-fight?

21. Go behind people to correct or reposition what they've done?

Of the items listed here, select two that are true for you and develop an action plan to effectively deal with them. Write down your plan here or on the worksheet you've printed out from the Website (*www.noexcuseguide.com*). When you've dealt effectively with the two you've identified, select two more and take action on these habits. Keep choosing two more until you're cleared your list.

## My Plan to Correct My Right-Fighting Habit

| Right Fighting Habit | Action I Will Take to Correct My Habit |
|---|---|
| Habit 1 | |

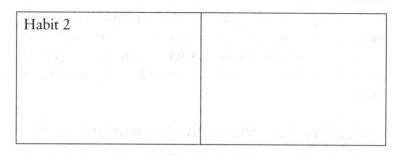

| Habit 2 | |
|---|---|
| | |

## Damage to Your Career

From a career perspective, the desire to always be right *is* toxic to your career growth and development. Not only do right-fight individuals drive away colleagues in formal office settings such as functional and cross-functional teams, but those with a right-fight reputation miss valuable (often office-political) information exchanged during informal settings, such as at the "water cooler," during office-sponsored events, or through informal, in-office conversation with colleagues. By refusing to consider the opinions of others, we shut and lock the door to new ideas and new possibilities.

> "The need to be right all the time is the biggest bar to new ideas. It is better to have enough ideas and for some of them to be wrong than to be always right by having no ideas at all."
> —Edward de Bono, physician, author, and inventor[5]

Unfortunately, for many of us, the idea that *we* are guilty of right-fighting would be a shocking realization. For many of us, right-fighting is a real self-awareness blind spot that works against us to hide our significant talents while preventing us from using our strengths at work. Even more tragic, this blind spot can destroy relationships with those whom we care about most. That's why it's so important to acknowledge this flaw in your personality and address it. Just the acknowledgment will open up new windows of thought, and you'll see yourself and other people in new ways that will lead to new opportunities for success and happiness. Vulnerability, humility, and transparency will become your allies.

## Getting Past the Right-Fight Blind Spot

Claudia Shelton is one of my business partners. She developed an assessment tool (*www.WhatsMyBlindSpot.com*) to uncover blind spots. I use the tool when I conduct leadership sessions for my corporate clients and EMBA students; it's an extremely telling exercise. Claudia told me during a recent conversation about destructive blind spots, *"I prefer to think of blind spots as the doors to opportunities that we are not yet able to see. When we think of blind spots positively, we open ourselves to the vision we need to gain the clear sight necessary to understand our blind spots and turn them into strengths."*

Do you want to increase your self-growth? Here's a start:

- Become more open-minded and willingly embrace the ideas of others. No frowning or raised eyebrows while you're doing it. Simply let go of wanting to be right. Let go of wanting them to see things your way. Let go of finding what's wrong with what they're saying.

- Focus on what they're saying, not on them. As you see yourself improving in these situations, you will also notice a certain calm that comes over you and a heightened level of self-esteem. Over time you will see that your need to be right will wane. You will have inner peace and calm. You will not be as serious. You will not be as defensive and dismissive. You will win a greater prize: improved relationships, both personally and professionally. And if you still have that moment of wanting to be right, it will vanish a lot quicker than it used to. Who wants to be right and lonely?

## Keys to Success

Many of the keys (to success and excuse elimination) I've been sharing in this book involve being selfless, supportive, and giving, and paying it forward. This topic is no different. When we welcome the ideas of others, we increase their confidence and our own, at the same time. The fact is those who desire to be right all the time are depending on others to supply them with self-esteem. Here's the real benefit of mastering the no excuse life and abandoning right-fighting: When we focus on *doing* right, rather than *being* right, our self-confidence and self-esteem expand, because we are no longer dependent on others for our own happiness. Imagine that! Now try this mantra (repeat it as many times as necessary):

*From this day forward I'm going to be more open-minded. I'm going to listen to learn, not to find fault. I'm going to lean in and not pull away. I'm going to lose sight of wanting to be in control. I'm going to embrace being understanding. I'm going to look for the wisdom in what people are saying and add it to my own professional and personal growth. I'm going to make peace rather than make points.*

### The Stop Right-Fight Rant

If you need some self-coaching to stop the right-fight habit, here's a personal rant you can use.

- *Stop right-fighting!*
- *Stop being so defensive!*
- *Stop taking things so personally!*
- *Stop thinking that everyone and every-thing is against you. They can't always be wrong, and you can't always be right.*
- *Stop being so angry—then calling it some-thing else.*
- *Soften up! Relax! Put down your dukes. Rest your mind!*
- *Don't use how you were raised as an excuse anymore.*
- *You are not your past.*
- *Shift your mind-set.*
- *It's totally up to you.*

I believe you can do it!

## Moving Past Right-Fight Reactions

So, you're committed to stop right-fighting and the ex-cuse behavior it supports. Great! Here are the four behav-ior reactions (adapted from Claudia Shelton's book, *Blind Spots*)[6] you're likely to face as you build your personal resis-tance to the habit.

### Anger

Anger can be a natural immediate response to disappointment. When we hold it for too long, we are stuck in that emotion and cannot gain an open or neutral perspective.

### Blame

Blaming someone else for a disappointment may be entirely justified. However, if you hold on to the blame, it means you're not taking responsibility and accountability for the goals you've set (eliminating right-fighting and improving the relationship).

### Withdrawal

Withdrawal provides a moment for recuperation. However, if you stay withdrawn, you are not actively working toward reaching your goals (eliminating right-fighting and improving the relationship).

### Knee-Jerk Reaction

The knee-jerk defensive reaction keeps us stuck in wanting to be right because it's a nonthinking response. If you don't get past this easy and predictable response, then you'll stay defensive and never shed the desire to be right.

## 7-Step "Stop Right-Fighting" Program

Okay, you've made up your mind! You're going to do it! Use this 7-Step "Stop Right-Fighting" Program to help keep you on course. I suggest you go to *www.noexcuseguide.com* and print out the worksheet. Post it on your wall or other visible place, and get started correcting these destructive behaviors.

1. **Recognize your own needs:** You probably have a strong desire to engage others in doing things professionally and/or correctly (or what you perceive to be the best way). In a fast-paced world, these standards can be over-looked and short-circuited—which you can experience as frustrating. Respect and do not lose your values and priorities for high stan-dards and quality. Respect and not just toler-ate, though, the values, approaches, and ideas shared by others, too. Refrain from showing annoyance and frustration when others don't share your opinions, approach, and/or atten-tion to detail (as long as it's not life-threaten-ing or hazardous to one's health).

2. **Help others to recognize your strengths and desires:** When necessary, help others real-ize that your input and/or professionalism is not meant to control them, but comes from a deep desire to build something or bring value for all (when this is indeed the case). Help others understand your broader con-cern, when applicable. Also articulate your interest in having others' input in develop-ing shared standards—not just assuming that your way is the best way. Show them that you are genuinely open and interested in what they have to say.

3. **Know your goal in any situation:** Given the situation, examine the goal you hope to achieve. Is it to be right? Is it to help? Is it to provide supportive information? Is it to seek clarification? Identify where it will be important to make sure your desire to be right does not get in the way of harming

the relationship or the outcome. Ask your-self in that moment: "What's my goal? What's my purpose?" If your goal continues to be "to be right," reread the chapter.

4. **Program flexibility:** If you are a leader, manager, or decision-maker and want to be seen as someone who empowers other members of your team, find ways to include others in setting values and standards for the way the team will operate. Individual contributors can use this approach as well. Be careful not to impose your "have to be right" sense of standards on others. You can use the same flexibility at home. Remember: You can win, and still lose.

5. **Express positive as well as constructive feedback by stretching your strengths:** When you operate in your "have to be right" mode, you may be seen by others as being inflexible, harsh, impatient, and overly critical. In addition, your strong style of communication may intimidate others, particularly those who are sensitive. They may see you as being hard when you are simply attempting to make a strong point. Where appropriate, engage others in conversation, rather than telling them what you want them to do or what you think. During feedback moments, listen with your third ear, and use your intuition and your sincere desire to help them to pave the way for enhancing their capabilities and level of self-esteem.

6. **Recognize early signs of shifting to right-fighting:** When you find yourself feeling

anxious, unappreciated, angry, isolated, and misunderstood regarding your desire to help, support, or clarify, realize that to other people it may seem as if you're trying to be right again. It's going to take people some time to adjust to your adjustment. Ask yourself in these moments: "Am I really attempting to help and/or am I whetted to the outcome?" When you give up right-fighting you can no longer be attached to the outcome. If people sense that you are attached to the outcome or that you're right-fighting, just without your usual intensity, this will still drive them away. People can tell a right-fight dressed as support any day. Also, are you looking for them to change, or are you willing to maintain your change? You could be holding inflexible or unrealistic standards for others to be agreeable to; this attitude can also create more distance than closeness.

7. **Learn to value the strengths and interests of those different from you:** Build partnerships and spend time with those who have different strengths, interests, and ideas than you to stretch your bandwidth. If you only know one way of doing, seeing, and approaching something, then you only know one way. Bring some diversity in perspective to your life. Remember: Giving up right-fighting is not merely being quiet to keep the peace. It's letting go of that desire to win and to control. People can right-fight quietly if they still have a right-fight spirit.

## STOP and START Personal Action Plan

STOP using these typical excuses for right-fighting:

- Someone has to be the voice of reason around here.

- I have to butt in; he's just so wrong.

- If you'd listen to me you'd see what I'm talking about.

- People just don't want to hear the truth.

START using these timely exclamations for eliminating right-fighting:

- I can lose and still win (the relationship)!

- I'm going to let it go; everything is not life or death!

- I'm going to appreciate other perspectives!

- From this day forward, my way is not the only way!

### START, STOP, CONTINUE DOING Habits

Now that you've given some thought to the problem of right-fighting as a way to rid your life of excuse making, add other **START Doing**, **STOP Doing**, and **CONTINUE Doing** habits that will help you attain this goal:

**Start**

## I will START Doing:

✓ _____
_____

✓ _____
_____

✓ _____
_____

**Stop**

## I will STOP Doing:

✓ _____
_____

✓ _____
_____

✓ _____
_____

**Continue**

## I will CONTINUE Doing:

✓ _____
_____

✓ _____
_____

✓ _____
_____

## Twitter/Facebook Affirmations

Post or tweet your one key takeaway thought, quote, phrase, or lesson learned in this chapter. Enlist your social network community of friends and colleagues to support your efforts to make positive changes in your life.

Make a note of your Twitter or Facebook post here:

_____

_____

_____

_____

_____

# Winning Way 9

## Avoid the
## "Taking Credit" Trap

*It's amazing how much can be accomplished if
no one cares who gets the credit.*
—John Wooden, Legendary Hall of Fame basketball coach[1]

Many of my students and workshop participants say this principle is really difficult to implement into an excuse-free life. That's easy to understand. After all, we all want (and deserve) to get full credit for our accomplishments—for example, getting published, being the first person in our family to obtain a doctorate degree, or finishing a marathon.

The "credit generosity" that Coach Wooden and I are advocating here is not an insistence on getting proper credit and recognition for our most significant professional and personal accomplishments. Instead, the kind of generosity discussed in this chapter comes from a deeper, more human place, and it requires you to develop a "spirit" of generosity that allows for the full inclusion and celebration of both shared and individual accomplishment. Unfortunately, we are not exactly "wired" to easily access our magnanimous or altruistic sides. In fact, most "base model" humans—that's likely you and me—come Matrix fully loaded with insecurities and fears that support and even encourage petty and jealous behavior. That's why we, in record-breaking speed, are in such a hurry to claim *all* the credit whenever and however we can get IT; it's also why we have the tendency to dole out the barest amount of credit possible to other contributors.

This chapter is essentially your invitation to join the Contribution Without Attribution Club. It's an exclusive club for two reasons. First, to be a fully vested member, you must truly celebrate both individual and shared accomplishment. That's not as easy to do as you think. And second, you must understand that another uniquely human tendency—excuse making—is what prevents us from enjoying the full benefits of a "share the credit" life. Don't see the connection? No? Then have any of these push-back excuses to the preceding discussion already occurred to you:

- "If I don't claim the credit, then no one will know that I've done all of the heavy lifting for the project?"
- "If management doesn't know that I came up with the idea, then how will I get the promotion or pay increase for my efforts?"
- "My time is too valuable to not receive credit for my ideas or work."

Do you see how these excuses are just cleverly construct-ed roadblocks that prevent you from even considering the possibility of a "greater good" approach to taking credit? Sure, you can make a good case for the practical benefits of tooting your own horn, and from a completely mercenary standpoint you'd be right. But trust me on this: Once you re-ally engage with the concept of a credit-sharing approach to your work and your life, you will be astounded at the results as you witness how this new alignment attracts more of the same spirit of generosity from others in your circle of col-leagues, coworkers, friends, and even family. (Yes, even your family!)

## A Personal Example

I met Brian Warrick in 2008. At the time, I had a fairly regular assignment with MetLife's information technology team in Bridgewater, New Jersey. Brian was one of the better presenters in my three-day, High Impact Business Presentations course, and we connected immediately. I appreciated his witty sense of humor (he now does stand-up comedy in New York), and he appreciated my high-energy, enthusiastic approach to capturing an audience's attention and for making your message stick with any audience.

Brian was also an Executive MBA student at Rutgers University. During an afternoon break, I told Brian that I thought my message of engagement and positive thinking would resonate with those like him who were in leadership positions. He agreed and offered to pass my business card and a five-star recommendation along to the EMBA program director, Dr. Farrokh Langdana.

Soon after that conversation with Brian, I was sitting in Dr. Langdana's Newark, New Jersey, office discussing the details of a formal relationship that continues to this day with the Rutgers's EMBA program. I even picked up another mentor (Dr. Langdana). That one, small act of generosity of spirit has given me the opportunity to teach hundreds of students in Beijing, Shanghai, and Singapore through Rutgers's International EMBA program. I have also been the program's commencement speaker, on their Shanghai campus, for the past two years. Moreover, I have been able to interact with, and form some powerful and endearing relationships with phenomenal students from more than 50 countries. Of course, these relationships have led to other international clients that help support my business and personal goals.

> Beginning today treat everyone you meet as if they were going to be dead by midnight. Extend to them all the care, kindness, and understanding you can muster, and do it with no thought of any reward. Your life will never be the same again.
>
> —Og Mandino[2]

Now, if you asked Brian about his part in the chain of events that led to such a fantastic opportunity for me, not to mention the bucket-list experiences I've had as a result of his simple act of connection, I guarantee that he'd minimize his role as much as possible. I've seen it firsthand. He refuses to take credit not because he's timid, or shy, or because he thinks his actions didn't really have any impact on the world. Nothing could be further from the truth. Brian refuses to take credit because he's strong, confident, and comfortable with who he is and the values he holds. It wouldn't occur to Brian to take an "I brought Jim Smith, Jr., to the Rutgers program" approach for my success (or anyone else's), because he is a member in good standing of the Contribution Without Attribution Club.

## What Do You Believe?

So, after reading about my experience with Brian, here are some questions for you to ponder about credit-sharing:

- Do you think Brian's credit-sharing sensibilities are unusual?
- Do you think he was born with such a sharing nature as a result of how his parents raised him?
- Do you think there's a genetic, predisposition for the self-confidence and strength of character one needs to share credit and celebrate the success of others?

- Do you think that for most of us such altruism is impossible and so taking an "if I'm not tooting my own horn no one else will" approach is your only option?

I asked a very successful friend (she's vice president of talent management for a top, Fortune Five consulting firm) about the importance of sharing credit. Here's what she said:

*In my mind, there is a real distinction between "taking credit" and being accountable for "building your own personal brand." If your mind-set is about taking credit, there is an inherent assumption of a zero-sum game...if another colleague gets credit then you lose stature. If you focus on building your personal brand, the assumption is that you have a set of unique skills and strengths that are different from other colleagues. It is in the organization's best interest that you articulate the value-add you contribute; what you stand for, your skills, passions, and attributes. Everyone has a personal brand, but they may not be conscious of managing it. Communicating a strong positive sense of yourself is a good thing for you and your organization.*

That's spot on, I believe, and it connects nicely with the actions you need to take in order to build a more generous, share-the-credit approach in your workplace and in your life. Here are some key brand questions for you:

- Are you communicating your brand, or are you looking for standing ovations to support your own insecurities and fears?
- Just what are you focused on?
- Are you focused on bringing value to every relationship and every interaction, or are you

focused on who's watching and how you'll be judged or rated?

What you choose to focus on is important, and it is directly related to how successful you'll be at sharing the credit or avoiding the tired, old, lame excuses for why you can't share or are afraid to share.

## How to Avoid the "Taking Credit" Trap

As I noted at the beginning of this chapter, developing credit generosity at work and in your life, on your way to a no excuse life, has the potential to be one of the most life-changing of the 10 "no excuse principles" covered in this book. However, developing this giving spirit is not easy; it will require hard work and perhaps significant changes to deeply ingrained beliefs and behavior patterns. And as my intuitive and sharp consulting friend pointed out, you've got to build your credit generosity brand over time and model its authenticity to everyone with whom you interact.

So, what do you think your brand might be? Have you ever thought about how those around you, see you? If you had to think about your brand in marketing terms, how might you develop it, package it, test it, project it, and live it? Consider the following next steps and questions about developing your brand.

Developing Your Brand:

- Ask your colleagues at work how you "show up" on the job.

- Ask your colleagues at work how your interactions with them make them feel or think about you.

- Ask the same colleagues to give you three *positive* behavioral characteristics and one behavioral characteristic you need to *polish*.

- Does your potential new brand align with your core values and beliefs?
- Do you live this brand both in and out of work?
- How will you reinforce your brand in both your professional and personal life?
- Think about what you want people to say about you when you're not around.

Now that you've got some idea what your personal brand is, you'll need to nurture and grow the seed you've planted. Part of the growth process is adopting the right attitude and seeking the right guidance. If you want the benefits of a confident, credit-sharing brand, then you'll need to look for advisors, mentors, coaches, or trusted colleagues and friends to provide feedback and help as you fine-tune your new brand.

So, where are you on your credit-sharing journey? Just getting started, or is it already part of how you conduct your life? The following exercise should give you a quick indication of your current position and the progress you need to make so that you can join the Contribution Without Attribution Club.

### —Credit-Sharing Exercise—

This exercise includes an assessment that will help you determine what changes you may need to make, to move you along the path toward sharing both individual and group credit. First, though, I want you to record a few recent experiences that demonstrate how you currently approach sharing credit. You don't have to make extensive notes. Just make some general notes about the credit-sharing situation, how you handled it, and your motivation for your decisions at the time.

| Situation 1 | What happened? What was your motivation? |
|---|---|
|  |  |
| Situation 2 | What happened? What was your motivation? |
|  |  |
| Situation 3 | What happened? What was your motivation? |
|  |  |
| Situation 4 | What happened? What was your motivation? |
|  |  |

| Situation 5 | What happened? What was your motivation? |
| --- | --- |
|  |  |

Do you see any pattern in how you approached these situations and the decisions you made? Give this some thought, and then take the simple assessment test that follows to see where you fall on the credit-sharing scale, from 1 (Member in Good Standing of the Contribution Without Attribution Club) to 10 (Credit "It's All About Me" Hoarder). Just put a check mark next to the statements that you think currently describe your approach to taking credit and add up your score.

## Assessment

☐   1. You always make sure you get the credit if at all possible.

☐   2. You get angry if someone claims and/or receives credit without including you.

☐   3. You make sure others know that you have a relationship/friendship with the person who's receiving the credit.

☐   4. You read the "thank you" list to make sure your name is included.

☐   5. You let people know what you've done or accomplished on Facebook, Twitter, or LinkedIn.

☐   6. You redirect the conversation so that you can mention what you've accomplished or the role you played.

☐   7. You will go back and correct someone if he omitted your name from the "credit list."

☐   8. You forward your customer "thank you" e-mails to your boss.

☐   9. You can sometimes sense that people become annoyed or agitated with you when you're taking the credit for something.

☐   10. You indirectly plant the seed for what you've done so that you can receive the credit without it appearing as though you asked for it.

Bonus (worth 2 points): You seldom feel appreciated or feel that people truly understand or value what you bring to the table (or to the relationship).

### Score

Give yourself one point per check-mark for each statement that applied to you.

1–3—Member in Good Standing

4–5—Acceptable, but Needs Improvement (be mindful of your insecurities)

6–8—Loves the Spotlight (probably got in trouble as a child for not sharing)

9–10 (plus)—Credit "It's All About Me" Hoarder

### What's Your Score?

What was your score? Do you need more work in order to join the Contribution Without Attribution Club? Whatever your score, the fact that you were honest enough to face the issue means a lot. After all, I'm sure you can think of co-workers who crave recognition and credit for simply waking up in the morning and showing up to work on time.

Maybe you know other, more productive coworkers (but no less annoying) who in fact do get a lot done at work, but spend an inordinate amount of their time focusing on who gets the credit, and considerably less time thinking about how they can improve and increase the value they bring to their department or the organization. You might even characterize these people as having a "reward expectation" attitude.

Of course, in today's work environment it is easy to understand the desire to get full credit. I often wonder if the interest in getting credit cuts both ways—in other words, are these same reward-hungry individuals just as eager to take the blame when things go wrong? Perhaps, that's a subject for later. For now, let's keep our focus on the credit side. Here's a final bit of hard-won and experience-driven advice: Stop keeping score.

Remember: When we give credit with the expectation of getting something positive in return, rarely does the good we expected materialize. Perhaps in the short run the reward will be yours, but over time, those who share and give credit based on a generous core value and spirit will always win, hands down.

## Priming the Selfless Pump

Avoiding the "credit trap" means we have to turn off our natural aversion to selflessness. As noted at the beginning of this chapter, we are not especially "wired" for this. Sometimes there are nice surprises and exceptions to the rule. Last year, I was running (okay, jogging fast) through the Houston airport to make a connecting flight to Phoenix, when out of nowhere, a white electric cart, with several other passengers onboard, stopped in front of me. The driver said, "Get in." He asked me where I was going and said he could drop me close to my gate. Thirty seconds later we were there! I hurriedly grabbed my bags, jumped off the cart, and sprinted toward the gate. In the far distance I heard, "You could have at least said thank you!" Really? I thought I had expressed my gratitude, but I guess I didn't say it loud or emphatically enough.

If you spend time developing a spirit of selflessness, you'll see it has great potential to enhance both your workplace success and joy in your personal life. How often do you get annoyed with your spouse or your friend when he or she doesn't say thank you for something you did? Are you doing it for the thank you, or because it's what you wanted to do?

My good friend, a Philadelphia videographer/photographer, Ken Frieson, describes the rewards of selfless giving: *"My life IS around giving and serving people—seeing that they are blessed in some way—that's my joy,"* he told me. *"I don't need a thank you.... The idea of giving without taking credit is a key part of* [my life] *professionally, personally and spiritually."*

> "Just a simple gesture of kindness — what possible difference could it make? Ah, there lies the mystery and the magic! Do we only give because we want an ego boost from knowing we 'did good,' or only when we get tangible proof that our gift will be put to 'proper' use? The beauty of unconditional kindness is that we may NEVER know."
> —Chelle Thompson, editor of Inspiration Line[3]

Another colleague and friend, Jim Brown, group sales manager at Greater Media Philadelphia, believes that wanting credit for everything is in great measure based on "fear" and "insecurity." As Jim put it to me: "[Maybe] *it's not having had enough of the 'love, reinforcement, accountability' balance when you were a child. Many of us just weren't grounded when we grew up. We've become selfish, self-serving and we lack character. We all need to have a greater purpose in life. My family motto is 'Do the right thing.' We all need to focus on being the best human being we can be."*

## Selfless Practice

So you want to practice being selfless to support your efforts to lead to a share the credit, excuse-free life? Then, take a few minutes and put a check by any of the following items that you'd be willing to do right now to accomplish that goal:

- ☐ Listen, not "one up" or interrupt someone; practice "listening with the third ear."

- ☐ Help someone with their career goals. It might just be as easy as passing along a business card to the right person or setting up or facilitating a networking opportunity.

- ☐ Offer to endorse the work of a colleague or friend you respect on LinkedIn or other social networking site.

- ☐ Help someone design/develop an upcoming presentation.

- ☐ Help someone with a computer problem even if you don't have time.

- ☐ Offer to proofread an important email, blog or article post for someone.

- ☐ Help someone out of an administrative support jam.

- ☐ Offer a colleague a ride to the airport.

- ☐ Encourage someone who wants to start their own company.

- ☐ Call someone to say "thank you!"

- ☐ Offer meaningful apologies and forgiveness for past transgressions.
- ☐ Tell someone they've done a great job.
- ☐ Alter your schedule to accommodate another person's schedule.
- ☐ Pick up the check at lunch for no reason.
- ☐ Offer business or marketing advice.
- ☐ Promote a respected and/or productive colleague to others.
- ☐ Reduce someone's workload for the day.
- ☐ Share a copy of your favorite book.
- ☐ Offer career advice.
- ☐ Tell someone how much they are appreciated.
- ☐ Offer to review someone's resume.
- ☐ Visit someone who you haven't seen in some time.
- ☐ Share a conversation with a loved one without, being judgmental.
- ☐ Do something pretty significant for someone and don't mention it to anyone else.
- ☐ Make a financial contribution to an organization in need.

Now, reread the list and identify someone who might need or appreciate your selfless gift. Write the person's name at the end of the sentence. If you can approach the task without expecting anything in return, then give yourself extra points!

> The majority of us lead quiet, unheralded lives as we pass through this world. There will most likely be no ticker-tape parades for us, no monuments created in our honor. But that does not lessen our possible impact, for there are scores of people waiting for someone just like us to come along; people who will appreciate our compassion, our unique talents; Someone who will live a happier life merely because we took the time to share what we had to give. Too often we underestimate the power of a touch, a smile, a kind word, a listening ear, an honest compliment, or the smallest act of caring, all of which have a potential to turn a life around. It's overwhelming to consider the continuous opportunities there are to make our love felt.
>
> —Leo Buscaglia, "Dr. Love," author, motivational speaker, and professor[4]

## Give to Live Challenge

Are you up for the "Give to Live Challenge"? For the next 30 days, I challenge you to journal your giving (without taking credit) experiences each day. Go to page 227 of this book or visit *noexcuseguide.com*, and you'll see the Give to Live journal pages. Record what you gave and how it made you feel. You will be surprised at the unexpected rewards that come your way.

## Give Back Surprise

Last year the Rutgers's University International EMBA program class of 2011 in Shanghai, China, asked me to be the graduation commencement speaker. I decided to keep this honor a secret from my students, with whom I really established a strong bond, and to surprise them with the announcement in person, at the graduation.

I did let a few students and business associates know, but told them to keep it a secret. When I arrived in Shanghai, I had a restful day one and geared up for my business dinner meeting with Frank, one of the students, the next night. Frank picked me up at my hotel and we took a taxi to the restaurant. When we arrived at the restaurant to meet his business associates (the carrot to get me there was other consulting work), he led me through the bustling crowd of dinners toward the back of the room. Unbeknownst to me, all 39 of my students were waiting. Their loud *"Surprise!"* greeting took my breath away as the emotion made my eyes fill with tears of joy. I got a welcome-back surprise party! The surpriser got surprised.

Later, I reflected on how this was such an awesome example of selfless giving. It took a lot of planning and coordination to pull off this surprise party. It wasn't expected in any way, yet this selfless act by my students created a memory I'll cherish for the rest of my life. They even sent me a video that showed how they planned the party during a break at one of their classes. Certainly, this outcome was better than giving in to all the excuses that could have easily blocked this memorable event from happening.

## STOP and START Personal Action Plan

STOP using these typical excuses for falling into the "taking credit" trap:

- If I didn't say anything, no one would know what I did.

- I made such a huge donation; I wanted people to know it was from me.

- I put a lot of time and effort into that.

- I'm not a "behind-the-scenes" person; I want and deserve the recognition I get for helping so many people.

START using these timely exclamations for avoiding the "taking credit" trap:

- It's not important who gets the credit!

- To whom much is given, much is required!

- I'm going to live to give!

- My new favorite question is, "How can I help?"

### START, STOP, CONTINUE DOING Habits

Now that you've given some thought to how you can avoid falling into the credit trap as a way to rid your life of excuse making, add other **START Doing, STOP Doing,** and **CONTINUE Doing** habits that will help you attain this goal:

**Start**

## I will START Doing:

✓ _____
_____

✓ _____
_____

✓ _____
_____

**Stop**

## I will STOP Doing:

✓ _____
_____

✓ _____
_____

✓ _____
_____

**Continue**

## I will CONTINUE Doing:

✓ _____
_____

✓ _____
_____

✓ _____
_____

## Twitter/Facebook Affirmations

Post or tweet your one key takeaway thought, quote, phrase, or lesson learned in this chapter. Enlist your social network community of friends and colleagues to support your efforts to make positive changes in your life.

Make a note of your Twitter or Facebook post here:

# Winning Way 10

## Live With Urgency and Purpose

*Let others lead small lives, but not you. Let others argue over small things, but not you. Let others cry over small hurts, but not you. Let others leave their future in someone else's hands, but not you.*

—Jim Rohn, speaker and personal-development expert[1]

Congratulations! You've made it to the last principle on your personal journey to a no excuse life. Like many journeys you've taken, your success depends largely on your preparation for the journey. Whether it's an extended vacation in Europe or a trip to the market to buy groceries for the week, preparation is essential. Forget your grocery list or didn't ask or text your spouse or partner about any missing items on your shopping list, and a second trip to the store is highly likely. Wait too long to make your airline or hotel reservations, and you'll likely be postponing that dream vacation, too. That's reality and, frankly, common sense.

Your success at implementing Winning Way 10 depends on how well you have prepared yourself as you worked through my other nine principles in the preceding chapters. Why? Because to fully engage with the true power of living with urgency and purpose means that every day you'll have to walk fearlessly onto the stage of life, find your mark, and face the blinding bright, no-place-to-hide stage lights, in front of thousands of onlookers and own your life. It's a full-time occupation. No room for excuses, blaming others, or procrastination—it's your show now and all eyes are on you (even if you don't think they are).

Winning Way 10 demands that you have the strength of character and resolve to move beyond your comfort zone— to drop self-imposed barriers and move past limiting insecurities and fears that may have trapped you your entire life, and engage with your life *now—full out* and *without apology*! Don't tell me that you're okay most of the time. That would be another excuse. And don't even think about suggesting what things would be like in a perfect world. Guess what? We don't live in a perfect world, and people are going to continue to remind you, based on what they do or don't do, that is the case. One of the rubrics I use in my seminars and workshops, thanks to my mentor Mike Jones, to help participants move beyond easy excuses to action is TAN (take action now). I constantly remind everyone that, contrary to what your dermatologist may say, working on your TAN is the healthiest way to live your life. In fact, working on your TAN is about the best way I know to rescue your dreams and goals from the "waiting room of life."

## My Call to Action

I hope this book, and specifically this chapter, will be your call to action—the needed catalyst to move you beyond the self-created bonds that shackle you to an unsatisfactory life. You will have to dig deep, and the experience might be painful, but I know it is possible and worth the effort. I know it is possible and worth the effort because I have seen this transformation happen to hundreds of my workshop and seminar participants, and I know it is possible because I have experienced that transformation and dug deep for the answers myself, and not that long ago.

A few years ago one of my major clients suggested that in addition to the training workshop that I was preparing for them, it would be beneficial if I participated in an upcoming leadership seminar in Houston, Texas. The idea was that I would experience what many of their current leaders had experienced, and this would give me a taste of the impactful training they were accustomed to. In fact, the experience did deliver on that promise, but as you will see, I certainly got way more than I had expected out of the experience.

First, no one told me—or maybe I just didn't understand—that the weekend retreat was a more motivational, live-life-to-the-fullest experience than just another "effective leadership practices" workshop. I guess I should have believed the Helen Keller quote that "Life is a daring adventure or nothing at all," on the seminar's Website. I quickly learned on the first day of the workshop that lectures and PowerPoint slides were not going to be part of this experience and that I was in for so much more. But before I tell you how all this played out, you'll need a little background information.

You see, I had arrived late to the workshop due to a cascading comedy of errors—all my fault and embarrassing, to be sure—that began when I locked the keys in my freshly acquired rental car after stopping at a CVS to ask for directions. (I know, I should have known where I was going in a Google Maps, everyone-has-a-GPS world.) In any case, my car key adventure resulted in my arrival at the workshop two hours late.

Right off the bat on the first day, we were asked to make a short presentation on a topic assigned by the facilitator.

You can guess what mine was: punctuality. Pretty mortifying, don't you think? I took the assignment in the spirit I thought it was given, and presented what I thought was a powerful and creative presentation. I was feeling pretty good about myself when I finished, thinking that asking me to make a presentation was like asking Emeril Lagasse to make gumbo or Diane Sawyer to report the world news.

The session leader made a few notes before I walked over to the facilitator's table to receive my evaluation sheet. She handed me my evaluation sheet and told me it was my grade for the assignment. When I opened the paper I was nearly floored by the big, red "F" staring back at me. I had failed my first assignment, and she proceeded, in drill instructor voice, to tell me and everyone else in the room why.

Three days later, I got a chance to redeem myself with another presentation. I was determined to nail this one. My assignment was to speak for five minutes on all that I had learned from the intense, high-energy, confrontational, high-risk, late-night, personal self-discovery leadership training workshop. I had learned that the reason for my first failing grade was because my presentation, in their opinion, lacked "passion, projection, and enthusiasm." I was determined to really show everyone "my stuff" this time. So, that's what I did. I gave the best professional motivational speaker presentation I could and sat down confident I'd get an A. But that's not what happened.

"Mr. Smith," the facilitator said, "You have to do it again and here's why. You probably thought since you're a professional speaker that you could just roll out one of your standard, rehearsed, inspirational presentations. No one is interested in a script! We want real passion and enthusiasm from the heart!" I was shocked and a little miffed, but I heard the facilitator loud and clear. So that's what I did. I threw away my script and dug deep for the next round. It was a painful and difficult thing to do, but I pushed past my own fears and found the courage to put it all out there. I finished with tears running down my cheeks, having touched something so real and raw in the process that I was simply exhausted.

When I gathered myself up, I looked at the facilitator and she smiled before saying: "Excellent, Mr. Smith. You got an A."

## What's Your Excuse?

What's your excuse for not digging deep? What's your excuse for not stepping over the line that separates you from the life you have and living the life you want? From my own experience, I had become complacent and maybe a little arrogant about how much I was engaged with my life. How about you? How much digging do you need to do in order to hit something real—something that might just bring tears to your eyes and create a life-changing catharsis if you only had the courage to face it? What excuse do you have for staying in your comfort zone?

### —Urgency and Purpose TAN Exercise—

If you need some help getting past the many barriers we all put up to avoid confronting difficult or unpleasant situations, I've developed the following three-part plan that may be just want you need. It involves your engagement with the complete contents of this book.

The first part of the exercise asks you to get "Excuse" feedback from seven people. Print the Excuse Feedback sheets from *www.noexcuseguide.com* and distribute them to seven people (for example, your colleagues, friends, direct reports, boss, or family members), and have them complete the form and return it to you. Tell them to be as candid as possible and that they don't have to sign their names, unless you want to dig real deep. (If that is indeed the case, schedule follow-up meetings with each person to discuss their thoughts. During the meetings you'll listen with your third ear.)

For the next part of the exercise, identify, using some of the feedback if you'd like, your most common excuses that keep you stuck where you are on your living life *full out* journey. The deeper the better. Take a few minutes to list these excuses now.

| | |
|---|---|
| Excuse 1 | |
| Excuse 2 | |
| Excuse 3 | |
| Excuse 4 | |
| Excuse 5 | |

Now that you've identified your most obvious excuses, it's time to dig even deeper. Here's a step-by-step approach that will help you accomplish this goal.

**Step 1:** Go back through this book and review all of your personal action plans. If you wrote your answers or made notes in this book, compile all of the exercises and notes into one place. If you downloaded and used the on-line forms from *www.noexcuseguide.com*, gather those electronic files and notes before moving to the next step.

**Step 2:** Make a list of the social networking communications you sent to others as you moved through the book. Gather the best of these thoughts and reactions to what you've learned, and post them someplace where you cannot avoid seeing your thoughts and promises (on your vision board, as your screen saver, on your exercise bike, or framed on your desk).

**Step 3:** Engage a "traction team." Ask coworkers or someone you trust (a friend, spouse, or partner) to help you build momentum and stay on track and meet your goals to live an urgent, purposeful, and excuse-free way of living. You can also participate with others on-line by signing up at *www. noexcuseguide.com* and by following the other social media outlets offered on that Website.

**Step 4:** Take a personal inventory of your negative attitudes and excuses. Focus on what brings you real inner joy; that's different from what makes you happy (such as a new car or a good meal). Joy comes from within. Examine the excuse habit in your life and how you use the habit to keep you from living with purpose. Is it chronic or just an occasional habit? Confront your fears by listing them on a piece of paper, and say out loud to shift your mind-set: "I'm taking your power away." Next, rip up the paper and throw it away. Remember: Challenges don't make or break you; they reveal who you are. Seek support for this self-examination using your traction team network (either in person or on-line).

**Step 5:** Join the "No Excuse Club" on the associated LinkedIn and Facebook pages. You'll find others there who have decided to take full responsibility and total account-ability for their professional and personal lives. You will find support from others who don't give away their power or let someone's opinion of them become their reality. You'll find many others who want to face any circumstance with confidence and without fear.

**Step 6:** Put yourself out there. Look for opportunities to get out of your comfort zone and use what you have found out about yourself using this book to succeed.

## The Rewards to Living *Full Out*

Clearly, there are many rewards for reinventing yourself and your attitudes. Not only will you have greater success at home and on the job, but you'll have time to consider what is really important in your life—what is essential to you. At the end of the day, it's really about the contributions you make in this life. It's about the hurdles you've cleared and the people you've endeared. It's about giving and giving some more. It's about evolving and growing as a person. It's about being "all in." It's easy to find excuses for staying on the sidelines and avoiding the problems that come with full engagement with your life and the lives of others. But is that really what you want to do? Is it? Stop reading for a moment and think about your life right now. Do you have work to do? Something you need to fix? Have an excuse that's been living with you for years? Here's some good news: It's never too late to start, and it's never too early. Right now, at this very moment, you get a chance to begin again. Up for the challenge?

Consider these perspective-shifting, accountability-driven questions, which I use in my Hot Seat exercise. I use this in my workshops and seminars to get my participants to find a sense of empowerment and personal responsibility, and to engage with their lives. Take a few minutes now and really dig deep to answer these questions. You can also download the form from *www.noexcuseguide.com* if you prefer to work on your electronic device.

### —*Accountability Exercise*—

I am most proud of:


My life goals are:

I have not been successful meeting my goals because:

Here are the positive changes I plan to make so that I will meet my goals:

I will ask the following individuals or take advantages of the following resources to ensure my success:

## The Person You Want to Be

Wouldn't it be great to be remembered as someone who never made excuses or who never blamed others? That's a tall order for almost everyone, but you can come close if you start now. Here's an exercise I use in my workshops to help participants examine the life they are living now and whether or not it's the legacy they want to leave behind. The exercise is called "What I Want to Be Remembered For." Essentially, I'm asking you to think about the meaning of your life—beyond the job you had or have (although that can be part of it). The exercise asks you to write a letter describing your end goal as a result of living a no excuse life. Really give it some thought and share it with others (your traction team, or friends and family).

You can think of the exercise as a project with a beginning date (today) and an end date. If this were a project the end date might be a completed building or the launching of a new product. In this case, the project concludes with a new you—an excuse-free you. You just have to connect the project milestones along the way to be successful. So here's your first milestone: Complete the "What I Want to Be Remembered For" exercise.

218 The No Excuse Guide to Success

*—What I Want to Be Remembered For—*

| |
|---|
| Date: |
| Name: |
| |
| What I Want to Be Remembered For... |
| |
| |
| |
| |
| |
| |
| |
| |
| |
| Signature: |

## Parting Thoughts

Remember: You are *not* your:

- Past.
- Job title.
- Credit score.
- Parents.
- Heritage.

And most importantly, you are not what others say you are! That's a definition only you have control over.

## STOP and START Personal Action Plan

STOP using these typical excuses for not living with urgency and purpose:

- What difference does it make? They already have their minds made up.
- I like things just the way they are.
- You could get in trouble if you're too enthusiastic. That's not our organization's culture.
- That's not how I was raised.

START using these timely exclamations for living with urgency and purpose:

- There is no time like the present!
- Tomorrow's not promised to anyone!
- Life is not a dress rehearsal!
- All we have is right *now*!

### START, STOP, CONTINUE DOING Habits

Now that you've given some thought to living your life with urgency and purpose, add other **START Doing, STOP Doing**, and **CONTINUE Doing** habits that will help you attain this goal.

**Start**

**I will START Doing:**

✓ _____

✓ _____

✓ _____

**Stop**

**I will STOP Doing:**

✓ _____

✓ _____

✓ _____

**Continue**

**I will CONTINUE Doing:**

✓ _____

✓ _____

✓ _____

## Twitter/Facebook Affirmations

Post or tweet your one key takeaway thought, quote, phrase, or lesson learned in this chapter. Enlist your social network community of friends and colleagues to support your efforts to make positive changes in your life.

Make a note of your Twitter or Facebook post here:

_____

_____

_____

_____

_____

# Conclusion

## Your Next Steps

Congratulations on finishing the book! Guess what? There's more work to do. I certainly hope that this book will provide the much-needed spark you've been searching for personally and professionally. Everything happens for a reason, and I'm sure there are myriad reasons why you decided to read *The No Excuse Guide to Success*. I trust that it will be a turning point for you and/or a wonderful reminder to continue to live the purposeful and "all in" life you've been living.

I've read a number of books (see Additional Resources on page 245) that have been "just what the doctor ordered" for me based on the life's challenges I was dealing with at that point. Considering my own experiences and numerous character-building moments, I promise you that if you apply the many principles I've discussed, continue to call on your accountability partners and traction team members, vigorously work your plan, and expect success, you will be able to live the excuse-free life you so desire and reap all of the benefits associated with doing so. I've seen it happen firsthand.

## Keep in Touch

The people who have attended my seminars and workshops continue to stay in touch with me, and share with me how much their lives have benefited and changed because they shifted their mind-set to remain focused on positive results and to take 100-percent responsibility and accountability for their behaviors and actions. Because of technology, I'm able to use Skype, e-mail, text, Twitter, Facebook, and LinkedIn to keep in touch with former participants who live in places like Oslo, Shanghai, Singapore, Istanbul, the Netherlands, the Bahamas, Beijing, Dublin, Kuala Lumpur, Kuching, and Bangalore. If you or your team members would like to take a deeper dive into excuse-free living, I encourage you to sign up for the two-day **No Excuse Personal Responsibility BOOT CAMP**. Just go to *www.noexcuseguide.com* to register. If you have others in your life who you think might benefit from eliminating their excuses, and you don't want to lend them your book (with all of your personal notes), please send them to *www.noexcuseguide.com* so that they can purchase their own copy and begin living a better, more productive, excuse-free life. Remember: Anything worth having is worth working for, and now's the time to work on your TAN (that is, take action now). You will never be the same. I know I haven't been!

## Your New Excuse-Free Life

Now that you've decided to change your walk, the fire is going to get hotter. People are going to challenge you to see how truly committed you are. They're going to say that your enthusiasm and dedication are going to wane. Let's prove them wrong and give them something positive to talk about. With that said, keep in mind that our world has changed tremendously over the past few years, but few have kept up. The way things used to be is not coming back. We now have different challenges, different audiences, different approaches, and seemingly less time and less support to accomplish all that awaits us. Our platters are full. Yet we still cannot afford to make excuses. Excuses stick out more than teenage acne.

So join the no excuses team. Lean into your discomfort. Put your discomfort zone up for sale. Eliminate your distractions and your distracters. Become good friends with vulnerability, transparency, fear, and ambiguity. Become more than a name or a face in the crowd. Don't be invisible. Roll up your sleeves and get ready for some hard, self-examining, life-changing work. Here's to your success! Enjoy the ride and take a lot of pictures! This is your *now*!

# Appendix

## Give to Live
## Journal Pages

# Notes

## Introduction

1. Carver, George Washington. 2006. Idea Finder Website, *www.ideafinder.com/history/inventors/carver.htm* (accessed 2012).

2. Franklin, Benjamin. ThinkExist.com, *thinkexist. com/quotation/he_that_is_good_for_making_excuses_is_ seldom_good/195979.html* (accessed 2012).

3. Nightingale, Florence. Famous Quotes and Authors Website, *www.famousquotesandauthors.com/authors/florence_nightingale_quotes.html* (accessed 2012).

4. Shakespeare, William. *King John*, Act IV, Scene 2.

5. Brown, Les. Mind of Success Website, *www.mindofsuccess.com/les-brown-quotes-the-power-to-change-1-of-5.html* (accessed 2012).

6. Wooden, John. John Wooden Quotes Website, *www.johnwoodenquotes.com* (accessed 2012).

## Chapter 1

1. Iacocca, Lee. ThinkExist.com, *thinkexist.com/quotation/people_say_to_me_you_were_a_roaring_success-how/261856.html* (accessed 2012).

2. Andrews, Andy. *The Noticer* (Nashville, Tenn.: Thomas Nelson, 2009), pp. 117–119.

3. "Man in the Mirror." Written by Glen Ballard and Siedah Garrett. Epic Records (1988).

4. Hairston, Rod Hairston. *Are You Up for The Challenge? Get What You Want in Your Life Starting NOW... Not Someday* (Leesburg, Va.: (Invictus International, 2006), pp. 26–27.

5. Ibid., p. 30.

## Chapter 2

1. Einstein, Albert. The Quotations Page Website, *www.quotationspage.com/search.php3?homesearch=albert einstein&page=2* (accessed 2012).

2. Hairston, p. 27.

3. Hicks, Esther, and Jerry Hicks. *Ask and it Is Given: Learning to Manifest Your Desires* (Carlsbad, Calif.: Hay House, 2004).

## Chapter 3

1. Horace. Successories Website, *www.successories.com/iquote/author/7460/horace-horace-quotes/2* (accessed 2012).

2. Neimark, Dr. Neil F. "The Fight or Flight Response." Mind/Body Education Center, *www.TheBodySoulConnection.com* (accessed 2012).

3. Ibid.

4. Ibid.

5. Truant, Johnny B. "6 Ways to Master Entrepreneurial Uncertainty." Copyblogger Media Website, copyright 2006–2011, *www.copyblogger.com/insecurity/* (accessed 2012).

6. Fields, Jonathan. *Uncertainty: Turning Fear and Doubt into Fuel for Brilliance* (New York: Penguin, 2011).

7. Jung, Carl Gustav. Good Reads Website, *www.go-doreads.com/quotes/show/50795* (accessed 2012).

## Chapter 4

1. Johnson, Stewart B. ThinkExist.com, *thinkexist. com/quotation/our_business_in_life_is_not_to_get_ahead_ of/12071.html* (accessed 2012).

2. Churchill, Winston. ThinkExist.com, *thinkexist. com/quotation/attitude_is_a_little_thing_that_makes_a_ big/219106.html* (accessed 2012).

3. Angelou, Maya. Quoteland Website, *forum.quoteland. com/eve/forums/a/tpc/f/99191541/m/2791905924* (accessed 2012).

4. Kuzmeski, Maribeth. *The Connectors: How the World's Most Successful Businesspeople Build Relationships and Win Clients for Life* (Hoboken, N.J.: John Wiley & Sons, 2009), pp. x, xiv.

5. Wooden, John. Goodreads Website, *www.goodreads. com/author.quotes/23041.John_Wooden* (accessed 2012).

## Chapter 5

1. Cavett, Dick. ThinkExist.com, *thinkexist.com/quotation/ our_business_in_life_is_not_to_get_ahead_of/12071.html* (accessed 2012).

2. Covey, Stephen. Legacy Coaching Website, *www. legacycoaching.net/quotes.html* (accessed 2012).

3. "Listening Skills: A Powerful Key to Successful Negotiating." HealthyPlace.com (America'sMental Health Channel), *www.healthyplace.com/depression/articles/listening-skills-a-powerful-key-to-successful-negotiating/* (accessed 2012). Article attributed on Website to "Roger."

4.  Roosevelt, Eleanor. Quotationspage.com, *www.quotationspage.com/quotes/Eleanor_Roosevelt* (accessed 2012).

5.  Churchill, Winston. Leadership Now Website, *www.leadershipnow.com/listeningquotes.html* (accessed 2012).

## Chapter 6

1.  Jordan, Michael. Inside Hoops Website, *www.insidehoops.com/forum/showthread.php?t=85251&page=4* (accessed 2012).

2.  Ghandi, Mahatma. Famous Quotes and Quotations Website, *www.famous-quotes-and-quotations.com/gandhi-quotes.html*.

## Chapter 7

1.  Jackson, Hardy D. Quote World Website, *quoteworld.org/quotes/7061* (accessed 2012).

2.  "Creating Employee Engagement." Assessments LLC, *www.mgassessments.com/employee-engagement.aspx*.

3.  "CBS Suvey: More Americans Unhappy at Work." CBS News Website, *www.cbsnews.com/stories/2010/01/05/national/main6056611.shtml*.

4.  "Why So Many People Stay in Jobs They Hate." *Small Business Trends*, March 16, 2011, *articles.businessinsider.com/2011-03-16/strategy/29977567_1_accenture-survey-employees-flexible-work-arrangements*.

5.  Ibid.

6.  Hanson, MS, Marlys, and Merle Hanson, PhD. *Passion and Purpose: How to Identify and Leverage the Powerful Patterns that Shape Your Work/Life* (Alameda, Calif.: Pathfinder Press, 2002), *www.motivationalpattern.com*, p. xvi.

7. Ibid., p. 3.

8. Ibid., pp. 22–3.

9. Ibid.

10. Ibid., pp. 35–9.

11. Ibid.

## Chapter 8

1. FitzMaurice, Kevin. Website of Kevin FitzMaurice, *www. kevinfitzmaurice.com/commu_argue_reality.htm* (accessed 2012).

2. *Merriam-Webster's Collegiate Dictionary, 11th Edition,* 2008.

3. Marston, Ralph. The Daily Motivator, *www.greatday. com/* (accessed 2012).

4. FitzMaurice, Kevin. Website of Kevin FitzMaurice, *www. kevinfitzmaurice.com/commu_argue_reality.htm* (accessed 2012).

5. De Bono, Edward. ThinkExist.com, *thinkexist.com/ quotation/the_need_to_be_right_all_the_time_is_the_big- gest/192825.html* (accessed 2012).

6. Shelton, Claudia. *Blind Spots: Achieve Success By Seeing What You Can't See* (Hoboken, N.J.: Wiley, 2007), p. 69.

## Chapter 9

1. Wooden, John. John Wooden Quotes Website, *www. johnwoodenquotes.com/* (accessed 2012).

2. Mandino, Og. The Quotations Page Website, *www. quotationspage.com/quote/31712.html* (accessed 2012).

3. Thompson, Chelle. SelfGrowth.com, *www.selfgrowth. com/articles/kindness-tolerance-diversity-life-quotes-to- empower-you-from-the-inside-out* (accessed 2012).

4. Buscaglia, Leo. Good Reads Website, *www. goodreads.com/quotes/show/41610* (accessed 2012).

# Chapter 10

1. Rohn, Jim. ThinkExist.com, *thinkexist.com/quotation/ let_others_lead_small_lives-but_not_you-let/324942.html* (accessed 2012).

# Additional Resources

Albom, Mitch. *Tuesdays with Morrie* (New York: Doubleday, 1997).

Andrews, Andy. *The Noticer* (Nashville, Tenn.: Thomas Nelson, 2009).

———. *The Traveler's Gift* (Nashville, Tenn.: Thomas Nelson, 2002).

Dungy, Tony, with Nathan Whitaker. *Quiet Strength* (Carol Stream, Ill..: Tyndale House Publishers, 2007).

Hairston, Rod. *Are You Up for The Challenge?* (Leesburg, Va.: Invictus International, 2006).

Hanson, MS, Marlys, and Merle Hanson, PhD, *Passion and Purpose* (Alameda, Calif.: Pathfinder, 2002).

Hicks, Esther, and Jerry Hicks. *Ask and it Is Given* (Carlsbad, Calif.: Hay House, 2004).

Jones, Mike. *Change Your Mind, Change Your World* (Houston, Tex.: Self-published, 2004).

———. *Unreasonable Possibilities* (Houston, Tex.: Self-published, 2011).

Kuzmeski, Maribeth. *The Connectors* (Hoboken, N.J.: Wiley, 2009).

Pausch, Randy. *The Last Lecture* (New York: Hyperion, 2008).

Peck, MD, M. Scott. *The Road Less Traveled* (New York: Simon and Schuster, 1978).

Redfield, James. *The Celestine Prophecy* (New York: Warner Books, 1993).

Shelton, Claudia M. *Blind Spots* (Hoboken, N.J.: Wiley, 2007).

Wooden, John. *They Call Me Coach* (New York: McGraw-Hill, 2004).

# Index

# About the Author

Jim Smith, Jr., is an empowerment/motivational speaker, trainer, and coach who has transformed the lives of thousands across the world, through his call to transform our lives from within. Some have referred to him as part–Joel Osteen and part–Oprah Winfrey, because Jim has a gift that enables people to overcome their inner fears and take their leadership, professional and personal development, and training and public-speaking skills to heights that were previously unimaginable. Individuals who have been JIMPACTED often leave emotionally drained yet inspired to reach new levels of personal success and make a positive impact to the world around them. His enthusiastic and passionate style of speaking has earned him the distinction of "*Mr. Energy*"!

Jim is the bestselling author of *From Average to Awesome: Lessons for Living an Extraordinary Life* and *Crash and Learn: 600+ Road-Tested Tips to Keep Audiences Fired Up and Engaged!* and the coauthor of *The Masters of Success* (along with Ken Blanchard, Jack Canfield, John Christensen, and others). As a personal power expert, Jim is also the creator of the acclaimed JIMPACT (Trainer, Facilitator) BOOTCAMP and The No Excuses Personal Responsibility BOOT CAMP. For more than 27 years, he has developed creative, inspirational, and high-energy approaches toward creating organizational and individual performance breakthroughs including his experience at the Bob Pike Group, Simmons Associates,

CoreStates Bank, the Vanguard Group of Investments, and Prudential's American Association of Retired Persons (AARP Operations). Jim presently serves as a faculty member for the Rutgers University International and National Executive MBA programs.

A sought-after trainer and speaker, his workshops, keynotes, and executive coaching experiences span across many industries, where he helps speakers, trainers, radio show hosts, managers, and leaders in how to deliver "mistake-free," memorable, and powerful presentations. His speaking style evolved, he says, from his ups and downs in Corporate America, education, professional and college sports, parenting, and marriage. It's this awesome journey that has taken him from a small second-floor, two-bedroom apartment in West Philadelphia, to JIMPACTing people from China to Chicago, Singapore to Seattle, and Turkey to Tennessee.

He lives in Mt. Laurel, New Jersey, with his wife Gina and their four children, and is a proud supporter of Autism Speaks.

# Also from CAREER PRESS

100 WAYS TO
MOTIVATE YOURSELF
Revised Edition
Steve Chandler
EAN 978-1564147752

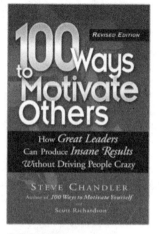

100 WAYS TO
MOTIVATE OTHERS
Revised Edition
Steve Chandler
EAN 978-1564149923

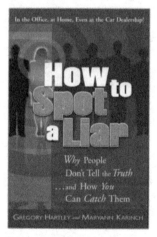

HOW TO SPOT A LIAR
Gregory Hartley &
Maryann Karinch
EAN 978-1564148407

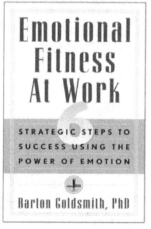

EMOTIONAL FITNESS AT WORK
Barton Goldsmith
EAN 978-1601630810